Magic & Miracles

Magic & Miracles

A WOMAN'S JOURNEY FROM DEATH TO DAZZLING

RITA BARBAGALLO

First published in 2022 by Dean Publishing
PO Box 119, Mt. Macedon, Victoria, 3441
Australia
www.deanpublishing.com

Copyright © Rita Barbagallo

All rights reserved. No part of this publication may be reproduced, stored in a retrieval system or transmitted in any way or by any means, electronic, mechanical, photocopying, recording or otherwise, without the prior written permission of the publisher.
Cataloguing-in-Publication Data
National Library of Australia

Title: Magic and Miracles: A Woman's Journey From Death to Dazzling
Edition: 1st edn
ISBN: 978-1-925452-34-1
Category: Memoir/self-help

This is an autobiography, the author has tried to recreate events, locales and conversations from his memories of them. In order to maintain anonymity of certain individuals in some instances names, occupations and places have been changed to protect individuals. Certain identifying characteristics and details such as physical properties, occupations and places of residence may have changed.

This book is a personal memoir and not intended as a substitute for the medical advice of physicians. The reader should regularly consult a physician in matters relating to his/her health and particularly with respect to any symptoms that may require diagnosis or medical attention. This is not intended for medical purposes or promote any particular type of treatment than that recommended to the individual from their own medical team— each person is different.

The views and opinions expressed in this book are those of the authors and do not necessarily reflect the official policy or position of any other agency, publisher, organisation, medical team, employer or company. Assumptions made in the analysis are not reflective of the position of any entity other than the author(s) — and, these views are always subject to change, revision, and rethinking at any time.

The authors or organisations are not to be held responsible for misuse, reuse, recycled and cited and/or uncited copies of content within this book by others.

Dedication

I dedicate this book to my loving husband and soulmate Salvatore CJ Barbagallo for being my rock, my lover, best friend and earth angel. For seeing in me what I didn't see in myself and helping me grow into the woman that I am today. Even in my dying days and toughest hours, you never gave up on me. I love you. You are my precious diamond; that rare, untouched gem that is unique and priceless.

Contents

Acknowledgements 9
Prologue 11

Part 1: Rita's Story

Humble Beginnings 18
What's Wrong with Me? 30
Beautiful Sal 42
How Much Can a Body Take? 53
Barbee Barb and Beyond 73

Part 2: The Rules According to Rita

10 Principles to Living Your Best Life 90
Resilience 92
Empower and Uplift Yourself 98
Dare to Be Different 114
Positivity 127
Embrace Life 140
Appreciation 149
Creativity 157
Optimise Opportunities 162
Courage 170
Kindness 180

Part 3: Rita's Parting Philosophy

The Future is Thrust Upon Me 188
About the Author 195

Acknowledgements

To my precious late parents, Francesco and Giuseppina Cirillo, for giving me life. You instilled in me a strong work ethic, morals, respect, generosity, and compassion for life and people. You taught me to always do the right thing. You were the wind beneath my wings and without your love and support, this book would never have been possible.

To my sisters, Angela, Assunta, Rose, Maria, Lina and Pasqualina; thank you for always believing in me, encouraging me to reach for the stars, and accepting me for who I am. I love the fact that we can always joke with one another and no one ever gets upset. We bounce off each other perfectly. It is amazing how we manage to always work together, through the good times and the bad. Thank you for always rallying together when I was sick. I appreciate every one of you, your husbands and partners. You are my rocks.

To my beautiful baby brother, Pasquale Cirillo. It is unusual to have a brother that I have always seen as my son. I cannot explain how protective I am of you, because I love you so much.

ACKNOWLEDGEMENTS

Maybe in another life we journeyed as mother and son. We are each other's lifelines; always there to pull each other up, and never let go. Your strength and resilience is something that I admire.

To my nephews, nieces, and godchildren, thank you. I love you all dearly.

To my friends in Australia who were the movers and the shakers throughout some of my darkest days, your help and support never went unnoticed. Louise, Estrellita, Margaret and Ron, Frances and Santo, and Helen, thank you all. Thank you to anyone I have inadvertently missed. A special mention and big thank you to Getrude Matshe, for all of your help, support and guidance.

To my overseas family and friends, Aunty Clementina, Uncle Antonio, Fernanda, Miranda, and all of the families in Italy. To my two childhood pen pals and lifetime friends, Stephanie Dehoust in Germany and Isabelle Weber in France, I would like to thank you for absolutely everything you did for me. I love and appreciate you.

To all the hospital staff, professors, surgeons, specialists, nurses, janitors, cleaners, kitchen hands, gardeners, and drivers of the ambulances and transport vehicles, I still remember all of you. You are just too many to mention. Please know that I still light a candle for you, up to this very day. Thank you for fighting to save my life so many times. I really appreciate you all.

Prologue

DEAD 16,700 KM FROM HOME

Have you ever died and come back to life? I have.

The first time I died, I thought, *is that all there is? Is it over? Am I dead?* I had suffered a heart attack and a stroke. My body shut down and I fell into nothingness.

There was no radiant white light at the end of a tunnel. It was nothing like that.

I was floating on the ceiling above my hospital bed. From up there, I watched on as doctors and nurses struggled to resuscitate the lifeless body below. They pumped it with morphine and pethidine, trying to coax the life back in.

The room was white – white walls, white sheets and white bedding. White uniforms were worn by the medical staff working busily on the ground. Stainless steel shone in every corner of the room. Hospital equipment beeped and buzzed loudly while the smell of disinfectant permeated the air.

PROLOGUE

PROLOGUE

Was that really me? Was that my body? I did not feel that I belonged to it, or that it belonged to me anymore. I was happy hovering above the bed – I felt no pain. I wanted to remain in that state and never return to my life; I had been in agony for such a long time.

Without warning, my focus changed. I was no longer in the operating theatre and found myself standing in a lush field. The breeze was cool on my skin as I wandered through the deep grass, tufts sprouting between my toes. I ran my fingers along the ground, the foliage soft and dewy. A cold crisp mist felt like the freshness of new snow.

I kept walking until I reached a white picket fence. Ladybird beetles rested on it, their red and black spots intense against the colourless palings. I felt like I was on the threshold of something, a final line that I had to cross over.

Beyond the picket fence was a large crop of tall sunflowers. I tried to reach out and pick one, but couldn't. I tried again. They were right in front of me – an arm's length away – but I was not able to touch them. Each time I stretched out through the fence, something would prevent me from plucking them. It was like an energy or magnet was holding me back.

With each attempt, my reach became shorter and shorter, until suddenly, the sunflowers disappeared. Everything around me faded and I was catapulted back to reality – back to the hospital and back into my body – where the pain started anew.

PROLOGUE

I begged to return. "Just let me go back there," I cried. "What do I have to do to go back?" I wanted desperately to return to that place of peace – to the field with the picket fence and the sunflowers. Of course, I couldn't.

We all say we don't want to die, but I am not scared to die if that is what death is. My life experiences have shown me that death is the other side of life and one cannot exist without the other. As long as you are six feet above ground, life is a gift, and is not to be taken for granted. We owe it to the universe to live it to the fullest.

Rita is sharing more in her INTERACTIVE book.
See exclusive downloads, videos, audios and photos.
DOWNLOAD it now at
www.deanpublishing.com/magicandmiracles

PROLOGUE

Humble Beginnings

Francesco Cirillo grew up in a small village in the south of Italy, where the sharp cliffs shot from waters made of sapphire. Villas dotted the coastline, sprawling up into the mountains until the earth transformed into craggy knolls of rock. It was a beautiful but unforgiving place, with the shifting seasons bringing with them a sense of uncertainty for all the villagers.

Like much of Calabria, Francesco's family was poor. The Second World War had devastated the region, leaving many of its citizens without adequate food, work, or money. At just 17 years old, a young and starving Francesco decided to run away in search of a better life.

There were two ships leaving the ports the day that Francesco left Italy. One was going to France, and the other to Australia. Whether it was his gut or divine intervention, something told Francesco to take the boat to Australia to start his new life, rather than settling further in the west of Europe. For three long months, Francesco and hundreds of his countrymen sailed across the world, hoping to be met with a better fate when they reached the shores of east coast Australia.

When Francesco arrived in Sydney, he had nothing but the clothes on his back and a few meagre possessions. For many years, he worked in the sugar cane industry and electric power transmission stations in Queensland, eventually returning to New South Wales and settling in Mangrove Mountain. He worked hard, slaving away throughout the harsh winters which by November had already morphed into stifling summer heat. He eventually bought a farm and cultivated the land, growing crops and rearing stock. It was a hard life, but Francesco was determined to build a stable future so that he would never have to starve again.

Back in Calabria, a 27-year-old Giuseppina was preparing to visit Australia. She was desperate to visit her older sister in Sydney, so she and six of her girlfriends set out on their once-in-a-lifetime adventure. Giuseppina bid her parents *addio* and boarded the ship. Little did any of them know that Giuseppina would never step foot on Italian soil again.

PART 1

Guiseppina landed in Sydney and by some act of fate, met a young man who had also come from the place she called home. They hit it off right away and the two were eventually wed. Francesco took his bride back to his farm on the mountain to start their life together.

Giuseppina had led a comfortable life in Italy. Her mother operated a doctor's surgery, so Giuseppina would spend her days exploring the city, or mulling about her mother's work. However, after marrying Francesco, Giuseppina was immediately thrown into farm life. She learnt how to drive the tractor, harvest the fruit, and slaughter the pigs. Together, Francesco and Giuseppina worked hard, night and day, to make ends meet.

Eventually, Giuseppina gave birth to her first child, a baby girl named Angela. Not long after, Francesco and Giuseppina welcomed three more daughters – Assunta, Rose, and Maria.

On 12 April 1968, a pregnant Giuseppina was hosting lunch on the farm. She had worked all morning preparing the glorious feast, and then spent the day entertaining 30 to 40 of her friends and family. At around 1 pm, Giuseppina finally sat down to eat and started experiencing severe pains. By the time the ambulance arrived, Giuseppina had gone into labour. Try as she might to delay the delivery, Giuseppina gave birth to her fifth child, a tiny baby girl, in the back of the ambulance. She named the baby Rita. And so began my journey in this world.

In my first few years, my parents graced me with three more siblings, my two little sisters, Lina and Pasqualina, and my only incredible baby brother, Pasquale. The ten of us lived in an old house on the farm, where five of my sisters and I shared a bedroom. A wide verandah fringed the building, that huge family gatherings would often spill out onto over the weekend. Through the week, mum would hang washing across long wires that stretched from one end to the other.

From the verandah, lush terrain spanned far into the distance. Thousands of citrus trees stood erect in careful lines, bearing their bright orange and yellow fruits. Massive gumtrees framed the perimeter of the property, where – depending on the season – the remainder of the land lay barren waiting to be seeded with potato, zucchini and tomato crops.

We lived a humble life, but we were happy. We never had the latest brand labels, clothes or accessories. It was always hand-me-downs. Mum would only buy us something new if we really needed it, so I would be dressed up in my older sisters' dresses and shoes. Sometimes our friends would donate bags of clothes to us. I didn't mind. Back then, those things were not important to us.

The exception was that we always had expensive food on the table. Because dad was in the primary production industry, he would barter with some of the different producers and suppliers that he had business with. In exchange for a fresh pallet of

PART 1

lemons, dad would take prawns, lobsters, and barramundi fish instead of cash for payment. Fresh seafood, mouth-watering cured meats, and decadent cheeses were always in plentiful supply at our house. Dad's mission was to make sure that we never went hungry like he had as a child, so he always made sure that there was plenty of food for all of us. It was the most important thing in the house.

Because my parents were farmers, my brother and sisters and I grew up working on the farm. We worked, picking fruit and vegetables, before and after school, on the weekends – basically every chance we had. From 3.30 pm to 8 pm, we would be out in the paddocks. Then we would have dinner, and if we weren't too tired, do our homework.

Every morning before school, us kids would take turns cooking breakfast for the whole family. We would get up at 5:30 am so that the meal was ready before Dad started work in the paddocks at 7 am. If we didn't get up in time, we would get a second chance to make breakfast the next day. If we slept through *again*, we would be punished and have to cook breakfast for an entire week! As well as cooking breakfast, we had to feed the chickens and the pigs and take out the rubbish before school. To take the rubbish meant a long walk down to the dump and back.

Finishing our chores before school was always a challenge. The bus would pick us up at 7:30 am from the top of our road, which was at least one kilometre away and uphill. Missing it was not an option. If we did, we had to stay home from school to work on the farm, and none of us wanted that.

As tough as the weekdays were, the weekends were harder. Saturday was market day, so there would be masses of fruit and vegetables to be packed. We had thousands of crops – tomatoes, lemons, oranges – to be loaded by hand onto huge semitrailers. We did not have any machinery to help us. Often, my parents would keep us home from school on Fridays to prepare. On Sundays, the big trucks would come in to take the produce to Sydney or Newcastle. Then on Monday morning, we would start all over again. That was farm life.

PART 1

Though we worked hard, we also played hard, and despite the taxing labour, life on the farm could be fun. I used to ride bikes. I had a bright green motorbike that I would tear around on – up and down the paddocks – to check on the livestock and crops. I was incredibly mechanically inclined, and was Dad's right-hand man when it came to servicing machinery on the farm. Dad and I would work side by side when something busted and needed fixing. I would watch him work, dispensing tools while I studied his hands coaxing the equipment back to life. Eventually, I could change a tractor tyre or repair a bulldozer myself, and took great pride tinkering away in my greased up used-to-be-white overalls. I ended up doing a mechanic's course at school and was awarded top of the class.

Sometimes, Dad would let us tie our go-karts to the back of the tractor while he drove through the paddocks. Through the grass we would zoom, swerving and manoeuvring away from any rocks or debris that might catch a wheel and tip us from our crate. On other days, Dad let us use his guns to practise target shooting. Each of us would have a turn trying to shoot down a series of little bottles that dad had lined up along the fence. We each learnt how to aim with precision and fire with calm, and were eventually able to hit one bottle at a time, without shattering the rest.

However, the fun was short-lived. Down the road from us lived a family with two boys, Neville and Alfred. One day, the brothers were toying in the garden, taking turns practising their aim and handling with the family rifle. Eventually, Neville retired to his bedroom, while Alfred remained downstairs with the gun. Unfortunately, the gun proved to be too much for Alfred, and he accidentally let it off, shooting straight up into the sky. The bullet soared straight into Neville's bedroom, killing him instantly. After that, Dad put a stop to us using the guns.

Tragedy was never far away for families of the mountain, and it was sobering for us all when it struck. On the farm, we had a swing made from a wooden soft drink box that hung from thick rope beneath two plum trees. All our friends had similar makeshift equipment, and there was even a rope version at our school. One day, my friend Kim and I were walking home after class. It was 7 pm and still daylight, the end of year warmth just starting to creep into what would become another season of endless summer evenings. When we reached Kim's house I said, "Bye, see you tomorrow!" and trundled off back to the farm.

At school the next morning, the headmaster mustered all the kids for an announcement. He told us that the swing in the playground had to be taken down – there had been an accident. Kim had been playing on something similar – made from just one piece of rope with a loop on the end to sit through – out the back of her house the night before. She had slipped and fallen through the loop, which became tighter and tighter around her neck until it snapped. Kim died – she had accidentally hung herself.

Growing up in rural New South Wales meant that trauma was around us all the time. We had friends who died on tractors and neighbours who ran their cars into tree trunks. Watching our parents slaughter the animals was enough to make any normal kid cry. We tried to cope with the grief as best as we could, but it was tough. It wasn't like we could go and talk to a counsellor about any of it. We had to suck it up and move on. If we couldn't cope, that was just too bad. Whether we suppressed it, or became desensitised to it, we grew a thick skin. It forced us to be strong.

THE BEST SCHOOL … EVER!

In the 1970s, I went to preschool. They were some of the best years of my life.

The school was like experiencing an incredible weekend, but we did this five days a week in kindergarten, and Grade 1. The school had about 30 to 40 students, and most of them were my family and relatives, with just a handful of friends. But one thing for sure was that we all knew each other very well.

My beautiful mother would arrive to pick us up on a tractor with an attached trailer (which would hold about 15 to 20 of us, if required), because she did not hold a driver's licence. In those days, it was acceptable to drive a tractor on the road, as we lived in a rural area, and all of the local houses had attached farms. In 1976 I remember there was a huge change in the school dynamics. The portable rooms were removed and many of the students were moved to another school about 25 minutes away up the road, because it was a larger school with more teachers, a library, and that school had about 150 children attending.

Now, we are coming to the best part of this subject. The school which my immediate family attended, was destined to be closed down, forcing everyone to leave. My father stepped in and called a parents' meeting. Subsequent to the meeting that night, the government decided to keep the school open and operational. Ultimately my father became the school president, with his four children continuing to attend; our close family friend, who also happened to be the godmother to my little sister, became the school secretary; the treasurer was another student's mother. So now we totalled ten kids in the whole school, and four of those were from my family, so school uniforms were not required. The situation lasted for four years.

We would play and do sporting activities every day, and occasionally, if our parents needed help picking fruit, we would all go and lend a helping hand on our nearby farm. While this was not too often, it was so much fun; I remember when all of the local schools would get together for a combined sports carnival, yet our tiny school of 10 children would clean up with ribbons. I was ultimately selected to represent the region at the NSW State Sports Carnival in 1979, and it was super exciting for me, the school and my family.

However, all good things must come to an end, and in the 1980s, the school finally closed, because it would have only had six children in attendance, so we were moved to the larger school up the road. Those were the good old days.

At my first school, we spent our time doing things like riding motorbikes, making art, and dancing the Canadian Three Step. It was pretty much just babysitting. It was very hard for me then, having come from such a small place, to compete with so many other kids in subjects like English and Maths – classes that we didn't do all that much back at Mangrove Mountain Public.

Then when I got to high school, I was completely shell shocked. I could barely read or write and I did not understand anything that the teachers were saying. To be honest, I didn't even know what a margin was until I got to year 7. I hated school. I would cry the whole trip in and dread going back the next day.

Although, I did excel in the sports world, and won lots of ribbons and trophies throughout both primary and high school. But year 7 I struggled, and during year 8 I avoided doing any schoolwork at all. It wasn't until year 9 that I actually started to enjoy going to class. My grades began improving, and I eventually climbed up from out of the D class, and into the A class.

My parents were impressed with my results. I told them I wanted to get a nursing degree so that I could work as a nurse after I finished school, rather than being forced to continue on the family farm. I was so excited. Finally I had a future – a purpose and a goal – that freed me from the shackles of the farm work that I had grown so tired of.

I enrolled in nursing as soon as I reached year 10. Every Thursday I went to nursing class, and afterward (instead of participating in school sport) I would walk into town for my shift at the nursing home. I loved it. After just six months, I graduated from my nursing degree.

Unfortunately, the dream was short-lived. Despite my parents' initial encouragement, Dad did not let me continue with nursing or even progress to year 11 or 12 at school. I was devastated. How could they do this to me? I withdrew from my family, spiralling into deep misery and anxiety.

I had no choice but to work on the farm full-time from that point on. It was gruelling. My sisters and I were as strong as adult men – lifting 100 kg wasn't hard for any of us. We were tough. We worked like dogs, night and day, just to make money to pay bills and get ahead.

What's Wrong with Me?

Growing up in a Catholic Italian family, my parents, and especially my father, were very strict. He always said to us girls, "While you are living under my roof, you do things my way. When you move out, you can do whatever you want. I don't care."

I loved my father very much, but growing up under such authoritarian rules was stifling. To go out and do something always required a chaperone, and even then we were only allowed to go after we had finished all of the work on the farm. If we did go somewhere, we had to look immaculate – like 'ladies'. We had to wear the stockings and the stilettos, ensuring that we did not show too much skin.

My dad had a deeply traditional way of thinking. He was petrified of something happening to us that would bring shame upon the family. After all, what if one of his seven daughters came home pregnant? What would people think? What if his only son got into a bad group of friends and started doing drugs? In his mind, he needed to control everything around us, in order to protect us. It was hard to accept at the time, but as I got older, I realised that this was his way of showing us love.

Our parents were very old school in their mentality, so it was no surprise that when I started experiencing problems with my period, that it was exceptionally tough on my family, as well as on me. Even though mum always made sure we were okay and did what she could to make us comfortable every single month, you didn't talk about that sort of thing back then. It was very hush hush. After all, it wasn't polite to discuss matters that should remain private between you and your 'time of the month'.

I had first gotten my period at 11 years old. It was 13 of September 1980 – Dad's birthday. I was out in the paddocks picking zucchinis when I sensed that something did not feel right. I looked down, and upon closer inspection, realised that I had become a woman. I raced up to the house to find my mother.

Mum was thrilled when I gave her the news. She gave me a big hug and helped clean me up, explaining what it all meant. That night, she sipped champagne in celebration of the remarkable occasion, as well as Dad's birthday. Little did she know of the horror that was waiting around just the corner for her fifth daughter.

My periods started out relatively 'normal', but with every month that passed, the worse they became. By the time I was a teenager, my periods were lasting weeks at a time. I could not understand how this was possible, when everyone else bled for just five or six days.

I began to endure months of excruciating pain. My stomach was like a hot red fire – burning with no end in sight. I would often lay on the bathroom floor where the tiles were cool and soothing. Day upon day I spent in bed, curled in a cocoon and cradling my stomach until the pain eased. When the worst had passed, I would feel fine for a few days, until it resumed anew.

On and on it went. My mother prayed that it would be over, telling me, "It's okay. It will pass, it's just womanhood." I asked her if everyone experienced as much pain as I did. Perhaps I was just over-reacting? After all, every other woman I knew dealt with their periods just fine. Maybe I was weak.

Many nights she sat at my bedside, stroking my hair while she cooed me to sleep. In the morning, she would bring me hot tea in bed, checking in to see if I was able to join the rest of the family for breakfast. I thanked God for her every day. She was my earth angel. My mum was what we would refer to in Italian as a 'piece of bread', because bread is something that you can't live without. I talked to Mum about absolutely everything. Even if she didn't fully understand, she was always supportive.

By the time I was 15, my periods were so bad that getting out of bed was almost impossible. I was in agony all the time. No matter how much medication I took, the pain would not ease. Regardless, I would be forced to work on the farm every day. I remember picking fruit and vegetables in the paddocks and being keeled over on the grass, unable to stand.

Even though I tried to make them understand, my family thought I was feigning, or at least exaggerating, what was going on inside me. They would call me a 'drama queen'. No matter how many times I tried to explain just how sick I was, they could not be convinced. They truly thought that I had made everything up just to get out of work. I felt like *The Boy Who Cried Wolf*.

I felt alone many times. No one believed me. I was forced to soldier on and work, despite the pain. I would spend hours every day pretending like nothing was wrong so that I did not disappoint my family. I was extremely anxious and depressed throughout this time – the pressure to push on and keep going was insurmountable.

PART 1

My family would say, "It will pass one day, when you get married and have kids." Even our family doctor told me not to worry, that it would settle down with time. After all, it was just a period. Periods came once a month and I would just have to deal with mine like everybody else did. Everyone thought they had the answer, but I knew in my heart that all their answers were wrong.

Eventually, I became so sick that I was taken to hospital. It was then that the doctors discovered what was wrong with me. I had endometriosis.

Finally, I had a diagnosis – a label from a medical professional that confirmed I hadn't been lying about what was happening to me. I felt validated. It legitimised what I was going through – that it was real. I wasn't weak, or worse – crazy.

My parents still didn't really understand what endometriosis was, so rather than resting, I continued to work full time on the farm. My body was under immense pressure from the physical labour. I never had a chance to recover or heal, so the pain from the endometriosis grew increasingly severe. I was in and out of hospital regularly, where I would undergo laparoscopies to burn off the tissue that had grown outside of my uterus.

To make matters worse, in the Catholic Italian community at that time, if you were unable to bear children, you were perceived as being less of a woman. As one of the most common side effects of endometriosis is infertility, I was left feeling incredibly isolated, afraid and vulnerable throughout my mid to late teenage years.

Eventually, my doctor recommended that I start taking the contraceptive pill. He told me that the pill could be used as a supplementary treatment, as it had the potential to mitigate my pain symptoms. The pill could also regulate and suppress my periods, which meant that the surgery I was having every couple of months could be reduced or stopped entirely.

However, there was a catch. The doctor would not prescribe me the medication without the consent of my parents. I knew that they would never agree, but I was anxious to try anything that could offer even the slightest bit of relief. Out of desperation, I begged my eldest sister to help me obtain the pill without our parents' knowledge.

I still get emotional thinking about the day I made that hopeless appeal to my sister. Like my parents, my sister held very traditional values. She assumed that my wanting the pill was so that I could have sex, and considered it outrageous that her unmarried little sister would even consider acquiring such a drug, let alone ask for her help to get it. No matter what I said, she refused to believe that the pill could help treat the condition that was tearing my body to pieces. She went straight to our parents and told them that I was trying to access contraception in secret.

Of course, my parents were furious. For weeks they relentlessly chastised me, incensed that I could show so much disrespect for them and for myself. If that wasn't enough, they then dragged me to our local doctor to discuss why the pill would not be administered to me, and that it was farcical for any GP to suggest otherwise. Shamefully, I sat in the clinic while Dad reprimanded the doctor. After all, the pill was only for married women, and not for any of his single daughters.

Despite this horrific fallout – and my deep hurt and embarrassment – I was not deterred. I had to try again to get this medication. I had three other sisters that I could potentially go to for help, but after what just happened, there was no way I was going to risk it with them. I had to get creative.

After I left school, I stayed in contact with my music teacher, Mrs Wolf. Mrs Wolf and I had become close during my final schooling years, to the point that she had given me her home phone number so that I could call her if I ever needed someone to talk to. Now seemed as good a time as any to take her up on her offer. My family had no idea about my relationship with Mrs Wolf, and I wanted to keep it that way. While my parents and siblings were out of the house, I snuck to the landline and dialled her number.

Mrs Wolf picked up straight away. For half an hour, she carefully considered my struggle. Mrs Wolf did not judge, she simply listened, interjecting only if she had a question. After I finished talking she formulated a plan: I was to see a gynaecologist.

I had no idea what a gynaecologist was, let alone how I was going to go and see one without my parents knowing. Mrs Wolf explained what I needed to do and where I needed to go. She painstakingly answered each one of my questions, no matter how pedantic or silly they seemed. By the end of the call, we booked an appointment.

I was grateful for Mrs Wolf's help, but she had created yet *another* problem that I was going to have to solve. The gynaecologist's first consultation cost $64.00. I didn't have that kind of money and I certainly could not ask my parents for it. They would be mortified if they knew I was even *considering* attending an appointment with someone who specialised in that kind of thing.

I was going to have to steal it. Mum would always take money from dad's wallet – whether it was some change for us kids or $100 for groceries. He never seemed to care or notice how much she took, so I figured this was my best bet at procuring the cash to pay for my appointment. When no one was looking, I snuck to my dad's wallet and warily thumbed through the money, extracting only what I needed.

I totalled $50 in notes and $14 in 50 cent pieces and stashed it in my bag.

My foolproof plan had gone off without a hitch, or so I thought until I heard dad questioning mum in the kitchen.

"Why did you take the money from my wallet?" Dad was not happy. He had put aside a specific amount to pay for something. When he opened his wallet and pulled out nothing but shrapnel, he knew immediately that the money had been taken.

My poor mum had no idea what he was talking about. "You must have counted it wrong, Frank," she said.

He lined all the kids up, interrogating us one by one. In succession we each told him, "No, I haven't taken it Papa."

Us kids were absolutely not allowed to take money from Dad's wallet without permission, and to our credit, we never had. Because of this unblemished record, Dad had no reason to believe that we had taken it now.

In the end, Mum got the blame. No matter how many times she tried to tell him that she had not taken it, and that perhaps he had counted it incorrectly, he was convinced that she was the culprit. I figured it was better her than me, so I let her take the fall for my crime. (He did eventually stop worrying about it and let it go, but there was still no way I was going to fess up.)

Eventually, the day of my appointment rolled around. My

mum, sisters and I went out shopping for the day in Gosford. After a few hours of retail therapy, I told them that I had to pick up something from another store, and that I would be back in half an hour. I dashed around the corner to the clinic, making it just in time for my consultation.

The appointment went well. It was incredible to be able to talk to someone who took my condition seriously and knew what they were talking about. The specialist explained everything I needed to know about endometriosis, before giving me a thorough checkup. Afterward, she wrote me a script for the pill.

I pulled out my purse and fumbled for the cash to pay her, handing over the notes. Carefully, I counted out the remaining $14, spreading the coins across the counter in towering bundles. "You can pay another time," she said, eyeing off the expanding piles of silver. "Or your parents can come by and settle the outstanding amount."

"No," I interjected, surprised by the volume of my own voice. "No one knows I am here. I stole this money to come and see you."

The gynaecologist was shocked. She lowered her eyes to meet mine and told me that I could come and see her anytime, free of charge. She said that I would not need to schedule another appointment in advance, and that I could just pop into her rooms whenever I needed to ask a question.

PART 1

I was grateful for her kindness, and ended up going to see her another six or eight times.

Because I wasn't well, and Mum didn't drive, Dad had to travel into town to pick up my sanitary pads and medications. Silently, Dad would accept my prescriptions and the long shopping list for the pharmacy and only return once the items were fulfilled. He never asked any questions and he never complained. Every week he would set off on his mission, driving for an hour and a half round trip to gather my various remedies.

About a week had passed since the gynaecologist appointment and Dad was ready to take his scheduled trip into town. As usual, I handed him my shopping list and bundle of scripts so that he could go and buy it all at the chemist. Only this time, I had slipped something else in amongst the others.

I sat at home in anxious anticipation, terrified Dad would discover that – as well as my usual medications – I had sent him to buy the pill. An hour and a half had passed when, like clockwork, he returned with the supplies. I sheepishly approached, half expecting him to scream out in rage with the knowledge of my deceit. Instead, he just smiled and handed me a bag filled with pills and hygiene products. *Had I gotten away with it?*

Another week rolled by and the same thing happened: nothing. Then another, and another. Every time he went to fill my scripts, I waited with bated breath, envisioning the pharmacist telling dad that his dishonourable daughter had been duping him into buying contraception. Fortunately, he never found out, and for years Dad continued to supply me with the pill without even knowing.

My dad was very tough, but he was honest to the core. Twenty years later, we spoke in detail about those days. All he could say was, "I'm sorry. I did what I thought was right, as your father." Even though things were tough, I could not get angry with my family when they truly believed that what they were doing was the right thing.

By the time I was 18, the endometriosis was so severe that it had attached to my stomach and was starting to spread. I had my first operation for what the doctors thought was appendicitis. It was then that we all discovered how severe my condition was. From that point on, I was in and out of hospital every couple of months.

Beautiful Sal

Have you ever met someone who is completely perfect for you? Someone who can lift you from your darkest day, or give you the strength to fight when you have none? Someone who brings so much magic into your life, you have to pinch yourself to make sure it's real? For me, that's Sal. My beautiful Sal.

I met the love of my life when I was 20. Now don't get me wrong, Sal is my rock. He is my precious diamond, my partner in crime, my best friend. But, I cannot pretend that when we met that it was love at first sight. It wasn't.

I was at my cousin's wedding, who incidentally was marrying Sal's best friend. I was all dolled up – hair done, heels on – when Sal saw me from across the room. He must have liked what he saw, because from that point on, he followed me around all night.

At the reception, he gazed at me from the table in front, eager to get my attention. During speeches, he shadowed me from table to table, following while I dodged his glance by switching seats with my sisters. All night we played cat and mouse – me evading his audacious pursuit. He was always in my face, trying to get me to notice him. In the end, I somehow managed to avoid him all night, and left without so much as saying hello.

About one week later, I was out on the farm greasing the Massey Ferguson tractor when a green Volvo pulled up. Out stepped a man, dressed in what could only be described as a *truly* heinous ensemble. He was wearing yellow shoes, yellow socks, yellow pants, a yellow belt, a yellow shirt and a yellow tie. He looked like a giant banana. It wasn't until I got up from the dirt, grease gun in tow, that I realised, *oh my God, that's that creep from the wedding!* He had tracked me down through friends and relatives at the reception.

Looking back, this is one of the most precious and beautiful memories in my life. However, at the time, I was completely weirded out. *Who did this guy think he was?* Despite my resistance, Dad told me not to be rude and that I at least had to go and have a chat with the guy – I was a lady after all!

My admirer returned again the next week, this time carrying 100 red roses. The attached card read: *Miss Rita Cirillo, if you don't give me a chance, you will break my heart.* I still have the card and envelope with all the trimmings that it was wrapped up in.

I had no choice but to give in to my better judgement and give the guy a shot. He told me that he was an accountant and played golf. We weren't off to a good start. All I knew was that crunching numbers sounded *painfully* boring and only old people played golf. He was straight laced – corporate and a bit nerdy – and liked to have everything in perfect order. Whether it was his appearance, his home or his car, his life had to be structured and organised. This was all in direct contrast to me: a larrikin farmer who rode motorbikes and took the mickey out of absolutely everything!

It was funny though, because despite our differences, the more I got to know him, the quicker I fell in love. After just three months, we were engaged.

We set a date for the wedding: 9 December. However, with every day that passed, the more sick I became. Unsure as to how much further I would deteriorate by the end of the year, we decided to bring the wedding forward to 5 August. We wanted to get married as soon as possible.

There was a lot of tension around this decision. My parents were confused and my sisters thought it was absolutely crazy that I was getting married so soon. Sal and I made a lot of changes to our plans, and our families did not understand why those changes were being made. There was a lot of doubt about our relationship. I don't think my family believed that I already knew that Sal was the right person for me. In the end, there was only nine and a half months between us meeting and getting married.

As the year progressed, I continued to bounce in and out of hospital. The endometriosis was growing quicker than ever before and I was not responding well to the medication.

A month before the wedding, I was in hospital for what felt like the millionth time. That is when they discovered it.

I had endometrial cancer.

That word: cancer. When I heard it, I was in shock. Back then, 'cancer' was only discussed once in a blue moon. No one I knew personally had ever been touched by cancer. Cancer was reserved for friends of friends – distant connections that I could sympathise with from afar. Cancer's poisonous grip could not reach my life. And yet, somehow it had.

I knew I was sick. I had lived with it every day since I was a teenager. But this was different. When I faced the reality of what the doctors were telling me – that I had cancer – it really sunk in. I knew there was a good chance that I was going to die.

I called Sal from the hospital and gave him the news. "I can't go into this with my family," I murmured into the receiver.

"However, we are going to get married soon and this is not looking good. I need you to come up tomorrow and speak to the specialist. Hopefully, we will be able to work this out."

I booked a consultation with my doctor for Sal and I. Although I had told Sal about the cancer diagnosis, I was worried that he didn't quite understand the seriousness of what *was* going to happen to me, and what *could* happen to us. I had to make sure that it was explained to him in medical terms by a doctor, because things were looking grim.

The two of us sat in one corner of the room, while the doctor explained what a diagnosis of endometrial cancer meant. The condition was undoubtedly serious, but there were options for treatment. Chemotherapy, radiotherapy – things that I never in my wildest dreams thought I would have anything to do with – were casually rolled off as run-of-the-mill remedies. I had been thrown into a whole new world, and I was scared.

When considering potential side-effects and outcomes, the doctor was very cautious. He did not say outright that I would not be able to have children, or that I was going to die. Instead, he prepared us for the uncertain likelihood of each or neither of those things happening. My prognosis was dependent on the effectiveness of the treatment.

Sal was unfazed. His stoicism was enviable – a vision of perfect calm and composure. Amazingly, he still wanted to marry me, despite being told that I might never be able to have children. "As long as I have her, I have everything I want," he told the doctor. Even more shocking was his reaction to the possibility that I might die quite early on in our marriage. "That's okay," he said. "Even if it's for a week, a month, a year; we are still going to get married."

It would have been easy for him to walk away. In fact, I told him many times to do just that. After all, I had no idea how long I was going to live for. We were both so young and I didn't want to lead him on, or have us living with false hope that we would start a family and grow old together. "Move on," I would say. "Just go and find someone that you can live happily ever after with." I look back now and think that if he had left me at that stage, it would have been devastating.

I was blessed to have met Sal when I did. I felt that I could tell him anything. He was my rock – my number one confidant. He did a lot of research about my condition so that we could better understand it. At my appointments, he would listen intently, taking notes of the doctor's advice. Whatever the doctor suggested, Sal would facilitate.

Sal had a special gift for assuaging my fears. He had a lot of faith. "We are going to be okay," he would say. "We will get through this." So, we did. We took each day as it came, trying not to think too far ahead.

I decided not to tell my family about the cancer. I did not feel comfortable talking about it with any of them. They

PART 1

already doubted me about the endometriosis, so there was no way they were going to believe that I had cancer. They would have assumed that I was too young to get it.

Meanwhile, preparations for the wedding continued as the date drew nearer. Two days before the wedding, my dad and I were levelling out the ground for a shed that he was planning on building. The earth was a beautiful bright orange clay surrounded by a field of orange trees. He was on one bulldozer and I was on another. We had just sat down for a tea break when he asked me, "You know, you're getting married in two days. Are you happy about that?"

These were not the sort of words that would ordinarily come from my dad's mouth. I was shocked. *Why would he say that to me, in this moment?*

It wasn't until the wedding when he was walking down the aisle and he said to me, "Rita, it is okay if you don't want to go through with this" that I realised why he was saying these things. I worked out that Dad, in his own loving and protective way, was trying to assure me that regardless of my unfortunate circumstances, he and mum would always be there to look after me – that I didn't need a husband to feel safe and secure. He was trying to reach out and support me, in the only way he knew how. *Did dad know more than I thought?*

Of course, he didn't. He had no idea that Sal had far more details about my health than he did. Sal and I were the only two who were completely on the same page. We both knew what we wanted to do, and all of the possible outcomes. Dad knew that I was sick, but I never told him that my condition could be terminal.

Despite my health concerns, we ended up having a beautiful wedding. I didn't care about all the frills and ruffles, leaving a lot of the decision making to my mother-in-law. The palette was bottle green for good luck, with the bridesmaids all dressed in satin gowns of the same colour. Folded red napkins marked each place setting on long tables draped in white linen. A huge wedding cake centred the room – decorated in red, white and green – that sat atop a brass cage containing two lovebirds that we released into the reception hall and flew around all night. It was very old school classic.

Though the early days of our marriage were filled with love and excitement, there was something looming beneath the surface that I had not dealt with. The last few years had taken an emotional toll on me and I was at breaking point. There were times that I felt so low that I could not regulate my emotions, and moments where I could not even force myself to smile. Often, I would be doing simple tasks, like watching television or cooking dinner, and burst into tears. I had no control over it.

Sal suggested that I get help. I attended a psychiatrist for my psychological symptoms, and a pain clinic to learn coping strategies to manage the pain caused by endometriosis. I was diagnosed with anxiety and depression and began a course of antidepressants. I remained on mood altering medications for another five years. Though I wasn't instantly cured, over time I was able to work through and address my unresolved trauma.

My family had no idea about any of it. In their eyes, to go and see a psychiatrist was probably worse than going on the pill! After all, only the insane saw mental doctors. Luckily, Sal did not see things this way. Instead, he understood the benefits of seeking mental health support, and made me feel at ease in undertaking treatment. Again, Sal put my best interests first, and together we combated my problems head on.

My life would not be what it is today, had I not married Sal. I would not presently be married nor would I ever have been married. I probably would not be alive. From the day we were wed and every day since, Sal has looked after me. He has always expressed his unconditional love.

My blessing is that I have a wonderful husband, like Sal. My husband is my rock. He is my rough diamond. I call him that because when you think of it, what is perfect? It is in the eye of the beholder. We are both perfectly imperfect.

You can't have it so wonderful in life with someone like

that, without feeling the need to give back. I believe that I have to work to make a difference to justify having a splendid life with my husband, living at home with the 'white picket fence'. The old maxim 'if it is too good to be true, then it probably is' does not apply to Sal. He is the exception.

How Much Can a Body Take?

Imagine poking a pin in a helium filled foil balloon and watching it slowly deflate. That was my experience with cancer. My body was irreparable.

Every time I had an operation, the cancer would grow back. It was like mowing a lawn – every four weeks you must go back and cut it again. It was a losing battle. The more the cancer grew, the quicker I had to go back to have it removed; by burning it off with a laser, or by other surgery. Parts of my intestine that weren't salvageable had to be permanently taken out in the hope that the cancer would not return.

Unfortunately, everything was just a bandaid solution. No matter what the doctors tried, the cancer kept returning. By the time I was 22, my specialist recommended that I undergo a full hysterectomy. It was the best shot I had at treating the endometriosis and cancer once and for all.

I knew in general terms what a hysterectomy would entail. It would mean having my uterus, and most likely my ovaries, removed. The short term side-effects – the bleeding, the pain, the recovery time – seemed inconsequential to what I had already been through up until that point. It was the impact that this operation would have on my future with Sal that left me reeling with despair and heartache.

I have always loved kids, and at that time in my life, having children was a dream that I held onto tightly and with desperate hope. I battled with myself relentlessly over this impossible choice. The cancer was killing me. There were no two ways about it. But a hysterectomy would bring with it a loss of menstruation, and in turn, an inability to conceive.

Hysterectomy or not, the chances of me having kids anyway were (at best) slim, but I could not eliminate the possibility entirely. I made the only choice that I could. I told my doctor to do everything he could to cure me, without resulting in a hysterectomy. I was not prepared to give up on our chance to have children until I absolutely had to.

My decision to decline the operation meant that the cancer spread to three parts of my body: the intestine, the bowel and the uterus. Eventually it spread to my stomach. It was growing fast and there was nothing that the doctors could do, because they didn't know what to do.

I grew weaker and weaker – slowly dwindling away. It was terrifying. At 23, I weighed just 39 kilograms. I was a walking skeleton. I had no appetite. The smell of food churned my stomach and made me sick. The only meal I could marginally tolerate was baby food, and even that was only on occasion. Back then, I could name every baby food recipe that stocked the supermarket shelf.

It was then that I made myself a promise. If I ever recovered, I was going to live my life with meaning. It was not going to just be about me – it was going to be about making a difference. From that day forward, I would make every single day count.

I had 26 operations in five and a half years and was in hospital on average every two months. Each stay ranged from five to 14 days. I was a lost cause. The cancer was aggressive and grew increasingly resistant to the treatment that was available. I was dying and we all knew it. We just didn't know when that final breath would be.

Eventually, there came a point where the doctors refused to operate. I was too weak and the operations were only prolonging the inevitable. There was nothing more they could do. It was then confirmed that I had just eight months to live.

Though my treatment up until this point had been the best in the country, Australia just did not have access to many of the leading technologies and procedures that international facilities were employing. Desperate to save me, Sal pressed my doctor to consider alternatives. As a last ditch effort, my doctor contacted the best specialists in Europe in the hope they could help me.

My first stop was France. I was examined extensively – poked and prodded – but the professor could not save me. I went to Germany. Same thing. My last hope was Belgium, where cutting edge treatment was being researched for my condition.

I met with a professor whose small team of experts had developed revolutionary material derived from pig skin to be used as a remedy for deep sores, burns, and to repair internal organs. Once the material was implanted, it prompted the body to replace the damaged tissue with little or no scarring. In my case, the professor proposed grafting the pig skin on top of the cancer which would stop it from growing. He told me it could save my life.

The catch? The procedure had only been tested on animals. It had never been attempted on a human.

What choice did I have? Worst case, I would die on the

operating table. Best case, I would be cured. I was going to die in eight months anyway, what did I have to lose? Despite the limited research, I decided that I would be Belgium's human guinea pig, for a chance at survival.

I booked a room for two weeks for my stay in Belgium, during which time I was to undergo various tests, ultrasounds, and bloods. From there, the medical team would determine whether or not they would be able to help me.

Each day that I attended the hospital was much the same – consultations and physical examinations. I would then go back to my hotel to sleep and, if I had the energy, explore the city surroundings.

One day, I woke up and left for the hospital for another consultation. As usual, I took my handbag and room key, expecting that I would return to the hotel later that evening. I entered the examination room and sat on the bed, restless to discuss the professor's recommendations and have some of my questions answered. He asked if I was happy for some other doctors to come and observe his work. "Of course," I said, "that should not be a problem."

For three hours, I lay there while the professor examined me, all while doctors, nurses and students breezed in and out of the room. Eventually, the professor asked, "Do you understand what we are doing?"

"Of course," I replied.

I had received so many needles, blood exams and physical check-ups, that I couldn't really tell one from the other. I understood that these were necessary so that the professor could work out whether he could help me. After all, he was a medical professional. I trusted him and assumed that everything he did was for the purpose of giving me the best medical advice going forward.

When the professor put the drip into my arm, I did not think twice. I assumed it was just another way for him to conduct further tests. I was wrong. Before I realised, I was put to sleep, ready to operate.

I woke up in theatre. I had no idea how many hours had passed. There was blood everywhere. Excruciating pain seared through my body while doctors circled above me in a panic. I felt life draining out of me. I grew weaker by the second, and then suddenly, it stopped.

DEAD 16,700 KILOMETRES FROM HOME

I was hovering on the ceiling, observing my limp frame below. The pain had melted away. I could feel the light sweeping over me, as peacefulness settled all around. I was finally estranged from my body, freed from the agony that had held me captive for years. I was dead 16,700 km from home, and I was happy.

My bliss was short-lived.

Eight minutes. That's all that had passed. It could have been hours. Or days. Time was an illusion.

When I returned to my body, the pain started anew. It was like a slab of concrete being thrown on the bed. Fire ripped through my body as the pain reignited. I found myself in the intensive care unit, fighting for my life.

The bed was made of hardwood. I lay there, covered in my own blood, haemorrhaging and needing help. I screamed for someone to come to my aid. Eventually, a couple ran over to my bed. I gave them Sal's telephone number in Australia and asked them to call him and let him know what was going on.

Distraught and alone, the worst was still to come. The doctors wheeled me back into theatre for a second operation. I have no idea what happened next, but I knew that if I survived, I would not be the same Rita ever again.

COMING BACK FROM THE LIGHT

"If you read her medical history, you would know that her specialist said she would not survive any further operations."

From my bed, I could hear a conversation between two

men. "You operated the first time without her knowledge, and have now created a massive problem."

A feeding tube jutted from my belly button. I had no idea how it got there. It was 12 millimetres wide and very long.

A drab sky of off-white panels stretched endlessly above me, extending further than my vision would allow. To my left, machines – buzzing and beeping. To my right, more machines. A small side table nursed a half filled plastic cup and a biscuit in a wrapper.

As I slowly absorbed my surroundings, I realised that nothing around me looked familiar. The men with the clipboards and the women in the blue scrubs were all strangers. The smell – clean yet sour – was foreign. It was obvious to me that I was in some sort of hospital. If the scenery didn't give that away, the searing pain running rampant through my body certainly did. But where *exactly* was I? And more importantly, how did I get here?

Before I had time to process how completely terrified and vulnerable I was, a tall man topped with a thick mop of dark hair breezed into the room. He wore dark grey and black clothing. *The janitor, perhaps?* I thought to myself.

The janitor asked me how I was.

Words escaped me. Even if I could articulate just how lost, confused, and frightened I felt, my mouth could not form the words. Nothing would come out. I lay there in startled silence.

Then, to my utter horror, he *kissed me.*

What on earth was going on?! If I wasn't terrified before, I certainly was now. My mind went into overdrive, searching for anything I could hold onto that would make sense of this madness.

"It's me. It's Sal," the janitor said. "I know you don't recognise me, but I know who you are. You are my wife. Don't you remember?"

I didn't. My mind was wiped, erased of all the memories and faces.

He squeezed my hand tightly. The warmth of his palm around mine spread to the rest of my body, like a hearth being stoked within. It calmed me. I felt safe, like he was here to help.

He opened a wallet and extracted a collection of photographs. Inside were pictures of me and him, and me and our dog, Candy. He took me through the pictures one by one while I tried to piece together what they meant, and who I was. I had my doubts, but slowly I started to trust Sal.

Eventually, Sal explained where I was and what had happened to me. I couldn't walk or talk, so I just lay there in complicit silence while he recounted the last few days of my life back to me.

I had undergone surgery to treat my endometrial cancer; a procedure that I never consented to in the first place. I suffered a stroke and a heart attack and died on the operating table. I was dead for a full eight minutes before I was successfully resuscitated. The doctors could not stop my bleeding and had to act quickly if they were to save me. In their haste to get me sewn back up, they accidentally left a sponge inside me, near the intestine.

When I came out of theatre, the doctors discovered that I had peritonitis: the elusive sponge had poisoned my blood. Just a few hours later, I underwent a second emergency operation to remove it. Again, I died on the operating table, but was brought back to life.

In between those two operations, Sal had received a call from Belgium telling him to fly over as soon as possible, because his wife was about to die. He had had to find the fastest way there. Several flights, a train, and 27 hours later, Sal had eventually arrived at the hospital.

I couldn't begin to imagine the thoughts that must have been running through his head: *How am I going to get her body back to Australia if she doesn't make it? What will I tell her family?* After all, he did not know whether he was going to find me dead or alive. After learning of the lengths he had gone to to be at my bedside, it broke my heart that I could have ever forgotten him.

Unfortunately, remembering my husband was just the tip of the iceberg. When Sal told me that I was one of eight siblings, I had a complete meltdown. Remembering one person was hard enough, but the prospect of having to remember another seven was horrifying. I was so confused. Whenever I saw someone new, I had no idea if I had met them before.

Under my father's instructions, an aunty, uncle and their two children flew from their home in Milan to visit me in the Belgian intensive care unit. When they arrived, it was clear they had not predicted the condition I would be in and had no idea what was wrong with me. After all, I had total amnesia and had all but lost the ability to speak – it would have made for quite a shock! To make matters worse, my aunty and uncle spoke no English, Sal spoke no Italian, and the doctors and nurses spoke little of either. In a way, it was actually comedic. Luckily, my cousins both spoke limited English and managed to help them all communicate, somehow.

My aunty had brought food with her. It was an Italian soup that I loved, made up of beans and different vegetables. The perfume of tomatoes and parmesan wafted through the ward. Something about that soup triggered me. As soon as I smelt the familiar aroma, I knew I was not alone. I felt warm and safe. Even though I did not recognise my family, I knew they were good, because I knew that soup.

Every day Sal and my Milanese family would talk to me for hours and hours. I took everything they told me with a grain of salt as I processed the information as best I could. Slowly, I started to remember things. Sometimes the memories were triggered by something that happened during the day, other times I would have a random flashback. Piece by piece my memory came together like a perfect jigsaw puzzle, over time.

If the amnesia wasn't bad enough, the stroke had left me completely incapacitated. I wasn't able to walk or talk – I couldn't even hold my own body weight. My arms and legs were like jelly. I had no movement or control over any part of my body. The medical staff would have to lift and position my limbs to where they needed to be. I was just a lump of flesh on a bed.

Day after day, the doctor told me to wiggle my big toe, and day after day I failed. Every few hours he pricked my knees and feet with pins in the hope that I would eventually feel *something*. But, nothing. I was told that I would never walk again.

My body was decaying – I was almost skeletal. The more medication I took for the pain, the more medication I had to take to stop the vomiting caused by all the pain medication. It was a catch-22. I looked up at my husband and murmured, as well as I could, "I am so tired. I just can't do this anymore. I give up."

"Don't be so selfish," he told me. "I have done everything

to keep you alive. You have to do it. If you're not going to do it for you, then do it for me." So, I did.

The doctor continued to stick his pins into my legs and my legs continued not to feel them. On and on it went, until one day, something happened. By some miracle, the doctor pricked my knee and I felt it! Better yet, the needle had actually *hurt* me! I could not believe it.

I still couldn't feel anything in my toes, but that didn't bother me so much now. I knew that the top part of my leg was working, which gave me hope that the rest of my leg would eventually come to the table too. The fighter in me returned. Two days later, I gained sensation in the top of my arms. Slowly, the feeling in my body was returning.

For the next three months, I was confined to a wheelchair as I struggled to learn to walk and talk again. It was as if my mind knew how to talk, but my mouth could not get the words out to voice them. I couldn't physically form sentences or express what I wanted to say. Similarly, I knew *how* to walk by watching other people, but I could not order my muscles to obey my mind. I was like an infant, starting from scratch on a very steep learning curve.

Once I became strong enough, the nursing staff would place me into a wheelchair and wheel me up and down the corridors of the hospital. When no one was looking, I would hoist myself up and stand, supporting myself on the wooden railing in the walkways. I recall falling many times and not being able to get up. The staff became angry and told me to stop trying. "You will never walk again," they said.

I refused to give up. Every day I would try again to make my legs work, and every day I would fall. Again and again I picked myself back up – physically and emotionally – until slowly I began to experience movement in my legs.

Eventually, I became strong enough that I was able to leave the hospital. We flew to Milan and stayed with my family so that I could continue recuperating. After many weeks, I was finally well enough to go home. We booked a wheelchair and two airfares, and set off back to Australia.

When we eventually touched down in Sydney, we were greeted by about 100 members of my friends and family. Cheering filled the terminal as Sal wheeled me down the arrivals ramp. One of my aunts came rushing up to meet me at the gate. She kissed and hugged me while tears streamed down her face. *Who is this crazy lady,* I thought.

Though Sal had taken me through everyone's name on the plane, none of it had stuck. I did not have the faintest recollection of who was who or how I knew them. I smiled and nodded as I got to meet my sisters, brother and extended family and friends again for the first time. It was like a movie.

For months, I worked at training myself to walk and talk. With every day that passed, the stronger I became. My

PART 1

memories returned in dribs and drabs. Eventually, I regained most of my basic motor skills, and could hobble around the house and fumble my way through a sentence.

As the strength in my legs and arms returned, I began experiencing numbness of my muscles. My limbs would cramp and shake uncontrollably. (I didn't know it at the time, but I later found out that I had the gene for Parkinson's Disease.) That's when the fibromyalgia kicked in.

My legs throbbed constantly. Applying pressure to them was the only thing that offered any relief. We didn't have bandages that I could wrap around my body and tighten with fastening tape, so instead, Sal would place old phone directories on top of me. He would stack me up with a bundle of them – one on each foot, each calf, and each leg, one on the side of my body, and one on my back. I had quite the collection. I would take a sleeping tablet and lie down on the bed with all the books on top of me to stop the aching.

The fibromyalgia set off a chain reaction and my whole body shut down. Over the course of the next year, I was admitted to hospital via emergency services on innumerable occasions. I was passing out at home, in shopping centres, on the footpath. Eventually, my private health insurance cut me off due to the enormous expense of all of the bills.

Then, the unimaginable happened: my period pain returned. The one thing I thought I was finally rid of was starting all over again. I was back to square one. My periods were lasting weeks at a time and I started vomiting up blood. I became anaemic. My internal organs stopped synchronising with each other and were under constant strain. There was a battle happening inside me.

I spent a month in hospital in Sydney. When the surgeons opened me up to explore what was causing the problem, they discovered that one of my ovaries had been removed, as well as six feet of my intestine. Not only had the Belgian doctors completely botched the job, they had taken out parts of my organs without my knowledge.

I didn't have many options left. After extensive discussions with the doctors, Sal and I made a difficult decision. Despite my young age and the possibility of never having children, the best thing for me to do was to undergo a full hysterectomy. There was no other alternative.

We kept the hysterectomy a secret to everyone. No one in my family knew. I thought that if people found out that I had had a hysterectomy, they would consider me a reject. In the Italian community at that time, it was frowned upon if you didn't have children. If you had a hysterectomy before you were married, then you would never be married. If you had one after you were married, then you were considered to be less of a woman.

Both of our families were eager for us to have kids, so

the probing was relentless. "When are you having kids? Why haven't you had kids yet? You are so good with kids!" On and on they went. No matter how many excuses we gave, the questions and judgements kept coming. I remember hearing my mother-in-law say to Sal, "If she can't have kids, leave her and get someone who can."

I still don't talk about it much with my family. It is hard for me to relive it, and it's hard on them to hear it. I know that I still have some family members who would consider me a barren spinster if they knew.

PART 1

It took me about six months to fully recover from the operation and hysterectomy. I continued with radiotherapy and chemotherapy for another year and was eventually given the all clear that the cancer was in remission. Finally, I could start getting my life back.

Barbee Barb and Beyond

While I was sick, I was asked to entertain a children's birthday party as Barbie Doll. After all, I looked like Barbie; I was very skinny, with long blonde hair and blue eyes, and besides, it gave me something to do. This became a regular gig. I would go to children's birthday parties and pretend to be Barbie. They loved it, and so did I. In those moments that I dressed in my pretty dresses and put on makeup, I felt good and whole. It was as if I was mending myself from the outside in. It energised me. For those brief moments, I forgot about my illness and pain, and focused on bringing joy to children.

When I performed, people did not know that I was sick. They looked at me like I was just a normal person. I started to think that if I don't look sick, I don't have to act sick. That changed everything. There was a massive shift in my vibration and inner wellbeing. That's when Barbee Barb Children's Entertainment was born.

Being one of the first companies in Sydney to start offering children's entertainment meant that I had a monopoly of the market. I was getting jobs left, right and centre and had bookings weeks in advance.

From there, I started building my empire. After just a few years I had a fully operational business and was looking for ways to expand my reach.

THE WAY OF THE WIZARD, MERLIN

I have been intrigued by magic since I was a young child. From gawking in disbelief as a man levitated before my eyes, to nervously watching a woman being sliced in two and put back together again, the mystery and wonder would leave me speechless. *How did they do it?* It was mesmerising.

I remember watching my first show; mouth agape and

spellbound by the theatrics. I was around 12 years old. My mother was lugging all eight of us (plus Dad) through the shopping centre while she frantically picked out groceries. As we left one store for another, I noticed something in the middle of the arcade.

Perched up on what looked like a big black box, were three young men wearing large top hats – two were dressed in black and red, the third in black and yellow. A grand backdrop of black and red stained curtains draped behind them. I watched on as they pulled a series of objects – a rabbit, a bunch of flowers – from a seemingly empty chest. I had never seen anything like it before. I was so overwhelmed I felt like crying.

Obviously, I *had* to take a closer look – I was entranced! I could not leave now just to go shopping with my mum! I *begged* her to let me stay. Surprisingly, but perhaps with the knowledge that we would not get the opportunity to see something like this again for a very long time, she let us watch.

That show ignited a fire within me, and my love for magic was born. I desperately needed to know how they had pulled off each trick! For weeks afterward I combed the newspapers and phone directories trying to find somewhere I could learn the craft, but there was nothing. Magic schools were non-existent. I ended up asking the school librarian about it and she brought in a few books for me. That's when my journey to become a magician really began.

PART 1

I studied those books cover to cover. Eventually, I started performing tricks at home for my sisters and brother. Sometimes, I would just perform for myself. I would spend hours crafting my props from whatever I could get my hands on: cardboard, rope, wire and string, usually. It was all consuming.

In the Italian community, the word 'magic' was taboo. It was likened to witchcraft, so I couldn't reveal all my tricks in case I was caught by my parents. Looking back, I laugh at how innocent I was and how harmless these illusions were.

One of my favourite tricks involved a bobby pin, an elastic band, and an envelope. First, I would bend the bobby pin into a sort of rectangular shape. I would then stretch the elastic band over each side, making sure it was taught between the two ends. Next, I placed a second bobby pin in the middle of the elastic and wound it round as many times as I could without warping the wire. I would then place the booby-trap into the envelope ready for my target. When the unsuspecting victim (usually my sister) opened it, the bobby pin would unwind noisily, scaring her out of her skin!

Though I enjoyed magic growing up, I never gave any real thought to practising it professionally. Until I got sick, it was just a hobby – something I loved that thrilled me and passed the time. However, when my condition began improving, I started to consider whether I was game enough to perform some of my tricks for the public.

I started watching how-to videos on performing magic tricks. Over and over I would replay the tapes until I could execute the illusion. Over a series of hours, days, and months, I gradually built up my repertoire until I could perform a handful of tricks to a professional standard. If there was ever a trick that I couldn't do because I was shaking too much from the fibromyalgia or the Parkinson's, I wouldn't let it stop me from performing the trick, I would just add another element to make it my own.

Once I was ready, I introduced magic to Barbee Barb Children's Entertainment and performed the tricks at parties. The joy painted on children's faces as they watched me pull a

PART 1

raccoon from a box or draw a stream of flowers out of a top hat was wonderful. All my years of practice were finally paying off!

Years later, I established the Barbee Barb Magic School. I started to teach other children's performers and kids with a passion for magic, like I had. My magic school, which I ran first from my home and then from my shop, has now been in operation for more than 20 years. I sell certain tricks and novelties at my shop for my students to purchase should they wish to expand their repertoire at home.

My students must all abide by the magician's code. The code comprises a number of rules that every magician must follow. These include:

1. **A magician must not reveal her tricks of the trade to anyone.**
   For a magician to reveal her tricks would shatter the magic for every other professional practising the craft. (However, I do enjoy showing children the basic tricks to get them started, and encourage them to learn the code themselves.)

2. **Magicians must always wear black, because black does not reflect light.**
   I really do not like the colour black, so I use it minimally. I prefer wearing red. Usually, I will wear a full red suit with sparkly red shoes.

PART 1

I have a membership to the Magic Castle in Los Angeles, an exclusive club for magicians and magic enthusiasts located in the heart of Hollywood. I go once every year and notice all the magicians dressed in their black suits and beautiful bow ties, looking weird, wacky and wonderful. Their ensembles truly are magnificent! But that is not me. I like to be different.

3. **Do not perform a trick unless you can do it perfectly.**

A trick must be precise for it to be performed, and therefore you must practise, practise, practise! I usually know once a trick is perfect, because I will test it on Sal. If he can't pick up on it, then I know that I have got it down pat.

Eventually, I started travelling around Australia teaching magic to organisations who were part of the children's entertainment industry. I would attend conventions and host events so that companies could learn tricks that they could perform themselves.

The joy of passing on a craft that is so meaningful to me, was, and still is, something that I relish. I continue to perform magic wherever I go. I love the joy and excitement it brings to every child and adult that watches my act.

Magic has a profound impact on those watching: the adrenaline rush, the mystery and the ability to pull things

RITA'S STORY

out from nowhere is transformational. Although magic is all smoke and mirrors, it is not just about the tricks. Magic is about creating a moment that can transport someone to a world full of hope, wonder and delight.

You don't need to watch a magician to experience magic. In life, we all have opportunities to create our own magic. It is all around us for those who know where to look. Some people see it and some people don't. Some people miss out living a magical life filled with mystery and wonder, because they are not in the present. They are so focused on things that may or may not happen, that they miss the magic moments that occur minute by minute, right in front of them.

DEVELOPING THE BUSINESS

Eventually, I started contracting out the children's entertainment. I no longer resembled Barbie, so I found girls who looked the part to perform parties and attend events. With my newly freed time, I was able to launch the Barbee Barb Collection.

The Barbee Barb Collection was born from a desire to create unique and bespoke products for women. I started by mocking up designs on paper with colouring pencils and then getting them made for my customers. Eventually, my designs and creations evolved into a full collection. If someone needed a customised clutch, pair of earrings, or shoes, they would come to me and I would make it happen. I loved making each piece unique for the client. After all, fashion is truly an expression of creativity and personality.

The Barbee Barb Collection was officially launched in Sydney in 2014. It has since expanded into a curated range that represents individuality, glamour and theatrics. The Collection embodies me, my journey, and my passion.

There is nothing I love more than seeing my designs out in the world. I have seen my shoes and bags on red carpets in Australia, the USA and internationally. I also offer styling services – which includes sourcing pieces, tailoring looks, and sometimes just being a shopping buddy – and have dressed celebrities for the red carpet and other events.

MAKING IT UP

After I got sick, makeup became a significant and valued part of my life. It was a tool I used to uplift myself when all I could do was lay in bed. When I was 'done up', I was powerful. I felt equipped to take on anything.

Even on my worst days, I still took the time to 'paint the canvas'. During chemo and radiotherapy, and even while I was on my deathbed, I would methodically apply my makeup, making sure that I took the time to go through the process each morning. When I was too sick to do even that, Sal would help me. Many times, he would visit me in hospital and paint my nails – even if he was just layering polish on top of polish.

Dad used to say to me, "You know what, because you always have your makeup on and your hair done, people don't even think you're sick!" It made me feel confident. Makeup had given me a sense of routine and normalcy when my life was anything but.

It might sound vain, but during those years, makeup gave me a huge part of my life back. I felt more motivated and in control when I popped on a bit of concealer and some lippy. It sounds ridiculous, but I actually felt *better* when I was wearing makeup.

This inspired me to do something new. A few years after launching the Barbee Barb Collection, I started to think, *why stop there? Why not make something that women can wear and enjoy every day?* So, during 2020, I decided to create and launch my own makeup line.

I contacted a lab in South Carolina in the USA. From there, I developed recipes for my products, including foundations, eyeliners, lipsticks, and mascaras. I crafted each formula from scratch, while I studied the science behind every ingredient. I made sure that all of the products were vegan-friendly and of the highest quality.

My products showcase my individuality. Each lipstick represents something or someone that is part of my life. From the shade 'Princess Brandi', a saturated peach liquid lipstick named in honour of my teacup Pomeranian, to 'Giuseppina', a stunningly bold fuchsia for my late mother, there really is something that showcases every facet of me.

My aim was to establish a product range that was not only versatile, but had the ability to make women feel beautiful and empowered. I truly hope that my products do just that. If I can help even one person feel better about themselves for just a split second, then I have succeeded in my mission.

MY HIGHER CALLING

Charity work has always been a big part of my life. I grew up working with charities, which was something my parents valued and indoctrinated me into. As I got older, and especially after I got sick, I dedicated as much time and resources as I could into helping those less fortunate than myself. Currently, I donate and support over 50 charities around the world.

One of the projects I am involved in is feeding the homeless. Once a week we set up in a park and supply food to people who live on the streets. As well as food, we also ask for donations of blankets, gloves, hats, beanies and socks and distribute them around inner Sydney. There are 10 of us that organise this.

Our team also coordinates shipments of supplies to go

overseas. The last order we prepared went to Zambia and contained toothpaste, soap and sanitary pads. The sanitary pads were handmade and reusable. We purchased material and sewing machines and sourced a number of volunteers who agreed to sew them for us. We had people making them from their lounge room – people who were retired or were out of work – and then we facilitated sending them out.

I also throw dinner parties to raise money for charity. At these events, I put on a multi-course, five-star meal with matching wines for small groups and corporate events. I usually sell tickets for anywhere between $3,000 to $5,000 depending on the menu, with 100% of the proceeds going directly to the organisation.

People sometimes ask me why I am involved with so many charities. To me, it's simple. If it wasn't for the Australian Red Cross, I would not be here today (they donated the blood for my many transfusions). If it wasn't for the Children's Hospital at Westmead, I would not be healed (they provided me with the plasma for my cancer treatment). If it wasn't for the support of St Vincent's, we would not have been able to access much of the treatment and assistance I required, including the wheelchairs I needed to keep mobile. I depended on charities and the goodwill of others to help me, when I couldn't help myself. I will forever be indebted to all of those organisations and individuals who gave up something of theirs, whether it was time, resources, or money, so that I could have a better shot at life.

I made a promise, in perhaps the most vulnerable, desperate, needy time of my life, that if I ever came out of that bed, I would dedicate my life to making a difference. I kept that promise, and I will continue keeping that promise until the day I die.

Rita is sharing more in her INTERACTIVE book.

See exclusive downloads, videos, audios and photos.

DOWNLOAD it now at
www.deanpublishing.com/magicandmiracles

Part 2

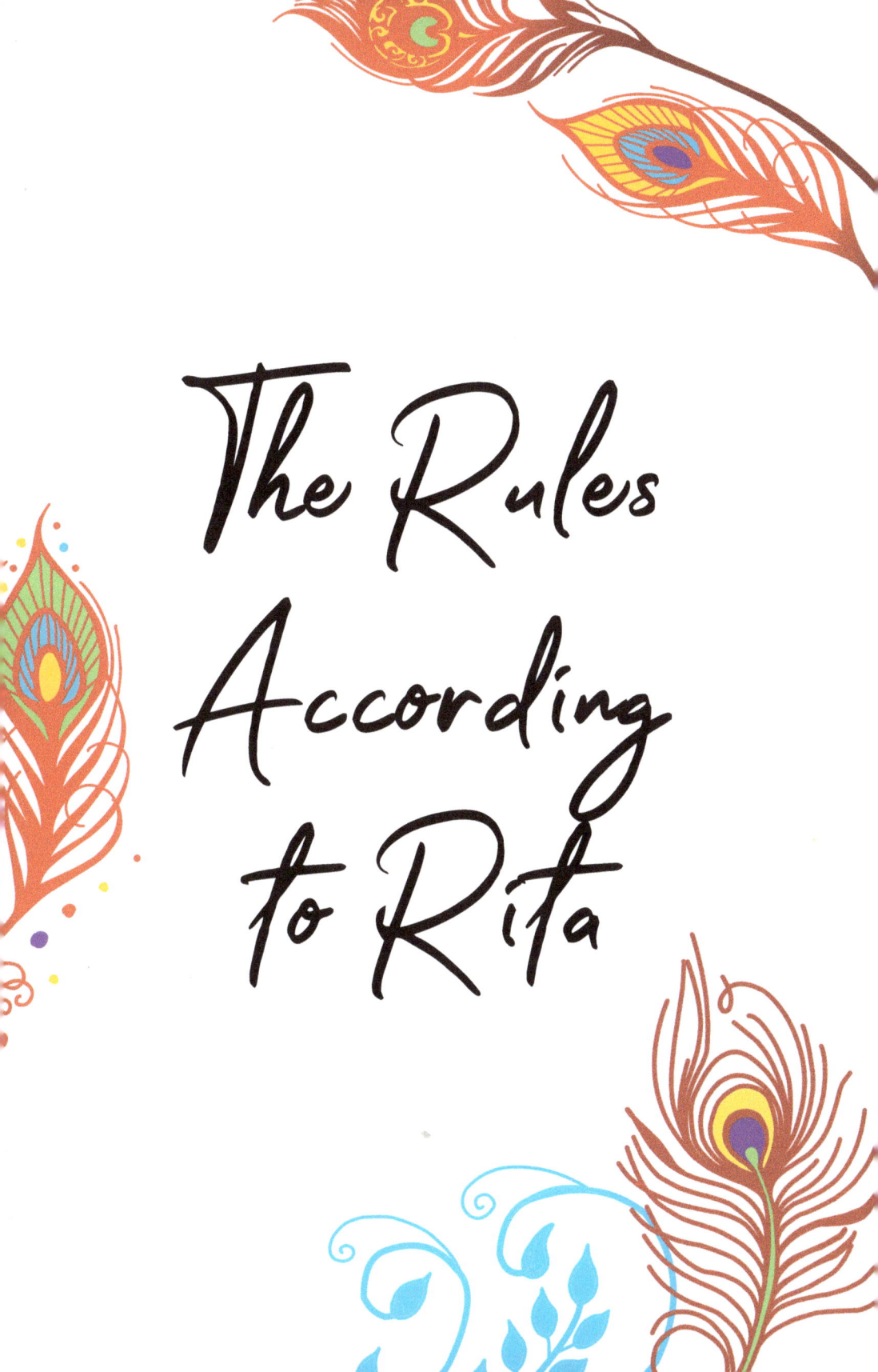

10 Principles to Living Your Best Life

In 2019, I launched myself as an international motivational coach and speaker. I wanted to share my experiences with the world, in the hope that my story could help other people in their lives.

After all, I don't think I was put on this earth to become

the greatest magician, the greatest designer, or the greatest entertainer. I know that I have a higher calling that I need to be here for. I have a job to do that I have not yet fulfilled. I believe that job is to help people.

My near death encounters have made me grateful and curious, so that I look for wonderful experiences in every passing moment. When a door opens, I walk through it, even just to see what is on the other side. Sometimes I take only one step and other times I am compelled to take one hundred. Magical moments reveal themselves at every juncture. I have found that this is a wonderful way to live.

Part 2 of this book delves more into how I choose to live, the philosophies that govern my decisions and actions, and ways that you can also achieve your best life. Keep reading to discover more! I've outlined these insights in my **RED PEACOCK** philosophy in this section: Resilience, Empowerment, Daring to be different, Positivity, Embracing life, Appreciation, Creativity, Optimising opportunities, Courage, and Kindness.

Resilience

I come from an old-school, headstrong Italian background. My ancestors were some of the strongest and most resilient people I have ever heard of. Providing for their large families was essential. They had a zest for life and could overcome any adversity that was thrown their way. It was this determination, strength and courage that was instilled into me when I was a child.

My father, through fortitude and perseverance, overcame all hardships in securing a better life for his family than what he had. Nothing could get in his way. He was a tough man, and from him I learnt to be strong and stubborn in the face of adversity.

If my father trained me to be unrelentingly tough, it was my mother who showed me how to be soft. My mother taught me that while strength was a valuable trait, gentleness and empathy were just as important. She lived her life with kindness, calm and tenderness, proving that resilience was not just about brute mental force – it was about so much more.

Growing up, I spent a lot of time cooking with my mother. We had a big copper barrel that sat atop a log fire which was used for boiling water. When we had a bath, we would have to heat the water in the copper and then carry it all the way back to the bathroom.

Mum would often wrap food in foil and place it beneath the copper, in the ashes of the fire. That is how she would cook. Eggs, meat, vegetables – she would bury it all within the embers, waiting until it was juicy and caramelised before digging it out for our lunch or dinner.

One day, when I was around 8 years old, my mother was cooking two chickens in the fire. After some time, she asked me to go inside and fetch her the oil and salt – the meat was ready and she needed to season the birds. As she reached down to pull out the foil packages, she placed two more sticks in the blaze. Without warning, flames shot up the wood, leaping towards her. The fire took hold of her dress, and within half a second, had it engulfed.

I had no idea what to do – I was just a kid. An entire hour went by before Dad got back from the paddocks. By then, she was completely burnt from the waist down. The nylon from the dress was grafted into her flesh.

Mum suffered severe scarring from the accident. It

still triggers me to this day. But she was a soldier. She never complained. She continued cooking for us kids and for her husband, despite her overwhelming fear of the heat and flames. It was impossible for me not to want to adopt her character after witnessing her cope so graciously. Nothing ever hardened her, but she was always resilient.

As I got older, the more I learned what resilience truly was, and it is now the cornerstone of who I am today. I have trained myself to bounce back and pick myself up, no matter what curveballs life throws at me.

Emotional and psychological resilience is your ability to persist through challenges that are thrown your way. It is not so much about your physical strength, as it is about the coping mechanisms you use to deal with a situation. When it comes to resilience, the power of your brain is more important than the strength in your arms and legs. Even if you can't walk or talk, like I couldn't, you will still be resilient if your mindset is strong.

Resilience benefits your life in many ways and can increase your emotional stability and relieve stress levels. People who are resilient are not thrown off balance when something does not go their way, and are generally more flexible than their counterparts who stick to rigid plans and rules. By 'going with the flow' and leaving room for error and change, resilient people do not feel overwhelmed when something does not turn out as planned, but can adapt to new situations more readily. This makes them less likely to become upset and overwhelmed when confronted with a problem, and more able to press through and tackle it head on.

Not everyone is born with the same level of resilience, and that is okay. It is never too late to start building upon your resilience. By changing a few key areas of your life, you will find it easy to increase your resilience over time.

POSITIVE PERSPECTIVE

Positivity is ground zero for resilience. If you have an optimistic outlook on life, you will not only find it easier to deal with challenges as they arise, you will also spend less time down in the dumps when something does go wrong. Positive people are able to see past immediate negative situations. They can see the bigger picture, and because of this, are able to reduce lingering feelings of pessimism and self-doubt.

Next time you find yourself in a 'negative' situation, try challenging your perspective. For example, rather than getting upset about having to stay at the office an extra few hours to meet a deadline, think about how great it will feel the next day, knowing that the task has already been completed. By actively altering your perception, you will become less impacted by adversities.

PLANTING THE PEAS

As a mindset coach, I use visualisation techniques to help my clients build resilience. In one of these exercises, I suggest using the image of a pea.

When you are happy and strong, take that mindset and imagine capturing it inside a pea. Then, take that pea and implant it into your brain for safekeeping. Next time you are feeling down or are having a tough time, release one of the peas. When you let it out, try to remember the good feeling that it represents. This will give you the strength to pick yourself up and dust yourself off.

For example, if I have to go to a function or dinner party and I have had a bad day, I will release a pea just before I walk into the room. That pea might contain a memory of a time where I was feeling particularly strong or happy. Because I know what that pea represents, I instantly feel better once it has been released.

Empower and Uplift Yourself

Did you know that approximately one in 10 women suffer from endometriosis?

It is a common condition that is often not spoken about, despite being suffered by women worldwide. For a variety of reasons, many suffering symptoms pre- or even post-diagnosis prefer not to discuss it. There is an inherent stigma and taboo associated with endometriosis, which often leaves people feeling like they can't open up about it to anyone.

As a disease that can only affect the female portion of the population, there is a common misconception that endometriosis symptoms are just 'part of womanhood' rather than being a valid and serious medical issue.

When I was growing up, I had a really tough time dealing with my endometriosis. As hard as the physical toll it took on me was, the emotional effects were just as bad. I struggled in trying to justify and explain the disease to my family, especially as I myself did not entirely know what was going on. There were times when I felt like I had no one: nobody understood what I was going through. For much of my late adolescence, I relied on sporadic medical advice and my own sense of what was happening and what to do about it. I did not have a true confidant that I could go to whenever I felt scared or confused. I felt completely alone.

Many people go through similar feelings and experiences, whether they are suffering from endometriosis or dealing with something else. My best advice is that if you are one of those people and you don't think that you can approach a family member, ask a friend, a teacher, or a trusted adult for help and advice. There is a good chance that someone will be able to guide you in the right direction. Just keep trying until you get the right help. You are not alone. There are also many support and crisis lines that you can call if you are in urgent need of help. Some of those Australian-based services are listed at the end of this book. The internet is also a great source of information and acts as a pseudo-confidant, when in crisis.

It took me over 30 years to reveal everything about my own struggle with endometriosis and be comfortable openly talking about it. Like many women, I was afraid of the judgement I might receive from other people, even from some of my own friends and family. I wanted to have a happy life, so why would I talk about it when I could just sweep it under the rug and pretend it didn't exist? After all, saying it out loud only made it more real.

It took me decades to shift from this mindset. But eventually, I slowly opened up and started sharing my story. When I did, it was like an avalanche of truth and a release of energy. I was suddenly unburdened and free.

I have now managed to divert and apply this energy and emotion to my philanthropic activities. This has given me the drive to uplift, inspire, and motivate people today. I strive to empower others, so that one day, they will be able to harness their strength and empower themselves.

WHAT I DO

I assist many diverse people in support groups all over the world to build better lives. I coach these people on mindset, resilience and self-empowerment.

My role is just to be a talking buddy. Those who I support can come and talk to me about anything and everything. I start by just asking basic questions, like how they are feeling and what they have been up to. I am a sounding board. It is my job to listen and help strategise ways that that person can accept who they are, and how to uplift and empower themselves.

I don't give medical advice. I am not a health professional. For this reason, I ensure that there are appropriate supports in place for each client so that their psychological and/or pharmacological needs are being met. I rely on other supports like psychologists and psychiatrists to assist from a therapeutic and medical perspective. I am just there to give my clients a confidence boost to illustrate to them that they are worthy.

A benefit of my work is that I can provide urgent daily support for my clients. Appointments with psychologists and psychiatrists can be expensive, so it is unrealistic that someone would attend these services more than once per week or fortnight. If I can lighten the load by assisting with my clients' day-to-day concerns, they can then take what we have discussed back to their counsellor for further advice. This multifaceted approach makes the process for everyone more efficient and leaves the client feeling thoroughly supported.

PART 2

SUCCESS STORIES

There is a group of women in Africa that I coach, pro bono. Once every two weeks, we get together on Zoom and they throw questions at me. A lot of the women feel more comfortable talking with me than with their doctor. So, after our discussions, I liaise with and relay the information back to their doctors, acting as the 'go between'. It is a beautiful thing.

I speak to one of these women at least two or three times per week. She is a medical officer in Zimbabwe who travels around Africa administering injections and medications to people who have been diagnosed with acquired immunodeficiency syndrome (AIDS). A lot of the women she treats are victims of rape, or their husbands engage with multiple sexual partners. Even though this woman is a nurse and medical officer, she too suffers from a serious condition of AIDS.

When we first started speaking, this woman was on the verge of suicide. Her husband had numerous sexual partners and she didn't know what to do about it. After many sessions, she started to accept that though she couldn't change the way her husband acted, she *could* change the way she responded in the situation. Eventually, she built up the courage to say enough is enough. Though she remains married and lives in the same room as her husband, she will not be intimate with him, or be intimidated by him.

Every person's struggle to uplift and empower themselves

will look different. A problem that may seem trivial to one person, may be a serious concern for someone else. An issue doesn't have to be bigger or harder than anyone else's for it to be important. Every problem is valid.

For one of my clients, her life looked picture perfect. This woman grew up with everything that money could buy. She lived in a gorgeous house with whatever she wanted at her fingertips. Money was not an issue. Her parents bought her cars, perfume – anything she wanted. She didn't need to get a job, so she had never had one.

At face value, this may seem like a pretty good gig. But despite having everything, this woman struggled severely with low self-esteem and self-doubt. Her entire life, she had been put down by others. She suffered from anorexia and bulimia. She was not accepted at school or by her friends, who all assumed that she was just a spoiled brat.

The first step was for this woman to get a job, which she did. I encouraged her to start saving. If she had any money left over at the end of the pay cycle, she could spend it on whatever she wanted. Under no circumstances was she to ask her parents for money. After a while, she bought her own car, moved out of home, and paid rent for the first time in her life.

Unfortunately, but perhaps unsurprisingly, her parents were not happy about this. They disowned her. After her parents cut her off, she was left nearly homeless, struggling to make ends meet for rent, bills and food. Still, she refused to move back home. Rather than letting her family control her like she had done in the past, she got a second job. She continued to struggle financially. So, she got a third job. Fast forward a few years and she is now thriving, living in a beautiful apartment with a successful career teaching music. She is independent, in control, and living a fulfilled and empowered life.

WORKING TOWARDS SELF EMPOWERMENT

Reaching a stage where you feel completely empowered might be the hardest thing you ever do, but it is not impossible. I have now worked with countless people who have been able to successfully recalibrate their thinking so that they can reach their potential and regain control of their lives.

1. **Love yourself**

   It is amazing the lengths we will go to to make other people happy. But when it comes to our own happiness, we often ignore our needs and consider them to be less than important. Why is that?

   We habitually prioritise the needs of those that we love, whether it be a friend, partner or family member. A lot of the time, our own happiness comes secondary. Of course, this can *sometimes* be a positive attribute. However, if you are finding it impossible to make decisions and take action that is solely in your own interests and this is affecting your overall happiness and wellbeing, then it is probably time to get empowered and take control of your life.

Are you prioritising someone else's needs because:

a. you are trying to be a nice person, *or*
b. you don't value your time and worth?

If you answered B, keep reading!

A lot of the time, the reason we can't improve our lives is because deep down, we don't believe we deserve to feel the happiness we desire. This comes from an innate lack of love, care and respect for ourselves. Therefore, it seems obvious to me that the first step towards self-empowerment is self-love.

Sounds easy, right?

Wrong.

Truly loving yourself takes time, patience and kindness. It requires dedication and perseverance. You have to find forgiveness and learn how to nurture yourself before you can really offer and accept the love you deserve.

Even once you have started accepting yourself, there will be days where you feel it is impossible that there could be anything about you to love. There will be moments where you doubt your journey – you will feel frustrated with yourself and want to give up. I *still* experience those thoughts and feelings at times. The road to self-empowerment is a tough one.

You will need to build a solid foundation of self-love. That way, if you hit a speed bump in your quest for empowerment, you have something strong to help you get back up and keep going. If you think, *I like this person, this person deserves to be happy*, then you will find it easier to act in that person's (i.e. your) best interests. You will be compelled to hold yourself accountable.

Mirror, mirror on the wall

An exercise I have my clients complete is to look into a mirror and tell me what they see. Every day, for 10 days, they must wake up and stare deeply at their reflection. They are not to leave the mirror until they can actually say to themselves, "I like you." By the end of the 10 days, they have to be able to say "I love you" and "You are enough".

I give them each a list of questions that they have to answer and give back to me. The questions specifically hone in on what it is that the individual does not like about themselves. For example, if someone thinks that they are unintelligent, I might ask things like: Why don't you like you? What are you seeing in the mirror that makes you feel that way? Do you think that way because other people make you feel dumb, or is it because you think that you're not educated enough?

The purpose of this is to work out exactly what it is that that person is unhappy with. Once we know this, we can map out a plan that specifically targets that issue (or issues).

By the tenth day, many of my clients will be able to say into the mirror "I love you because you are enough." This is a great achievement. Of course, the journey does not stop there. The client needs to consistently build upon that foundation to reinforce that they are loveable, capable and worthy. They must ingrain it into themselves that they deserve to be happy and achieve their goals.

Equally, there are a lot of clients who won't be able to do it. For some, it will take three or four days to even look at themselves in the mirror. For these people, they may need to work through the exercise over a series of weeks, rather than just the standard 10 days. It is important that they also utilise the professional help available from their therapeutic supports.

Your turn!
a. Look into a mirror.
b. Think about what it is that you don't love about yourself and write it down.
c. Consider what it is that makes you feel that way.
d. What can you do to change the way you feel about yourself? Put these things into a list.
e. Accept yourself by saying "I love you" into the mirror.
f. Repeat the exercise for 10 days. After each day, you will delve into your feelings and issues a little deeper. (By the tenth day, you may discover that the root of your self criticism stems from an entirely different issue than you initially thought.)

7. A good deed a day

'My way to play is to do a good deed a day' is a motto I live by.

Doing something for someone else will not only positively impact that person's day, but can also bring a smile to your dial and reward you with an uplifting feeling of gratitude. This is because when you do a good deed, your brain releases endorphins – a happy hormone. When you give back, your heart is singing.

I always encourage my clients to take on a task that will empower and uplift someone else. It doesn't have to be monetary. Even the smallest acts of kindness will produce rewards for you and the other person. The more good deeds you do, the more light you will bring to your life and those around you.

Some simple examples include:
a. Holding the door open for someone.
b. Letting someone in front of you in the shopping line.
c. Paying it forward at your local coffee shop.
d. Completing household chores for the people you live with.
e. Sending a gift to a loved one.
f. Volunteering your time at a charitable or not-for-profit organisation.
g. Donating money or items to charity.

There is no limit to the ways in which you can help others. Get creative. Every day, I must do at least one good deed for someone else. If I don't, I cannot go to bed because it means that I have not completed my day.

8. **Step outside the comfort zone**
Many of my clients practise stepping outside of their comfort zones as a strategy to develop self-empowerment. The objective is that they confront and conquer the fears

that inhibit them taking control of their lives.

Because everyone's 'comfort zone' is different, there is no 'one size fits all' exercise for this. Something that is easy for one person might be near impossible for the next.

For example, some of the women I coach have been mentally, physically and emotionally abused. As a result, they are unable to communicate with unfamiliar men. For one woman, this has meant that she has never been able to fill her car with petrol; either her husband or her son must do it. One day she was driving alone and needed to refuel. She called me in a panic, saying that she didn't know what to do because she couldn't fill up the car herself. I spent some time reassuring her and talking her through it. Eventually, she filled up the car. Anxiously, she then entered the service station, walked to the counter, and paid the male attendant for the fuel. This took an enormous amount of courage and was a huge leap toward crushing one of her biggest fears.

Another woman that I coach told me that, due to her acute agoraphobia, it had been years since she had last sat in a café and enjoyed a coffee. So, I assigned her the challenge of ordering a latte and sitting in a coffee shop for one whole hour. This was extremely difficult for her. Each time she attempted the task, she got that little bit closer, but ultimately backed out. After three or four attempts, she eventually succeeded.

For both women, completing these tasks didn't instantly cure them of their phobias. However, it did incite enough confidence and self-esteem that they could continue to push themselves outside of their comfort zones. Eventually, little by little, they felt secure enough to complete these tasks with ease. The more they practised, the closer they got to taking back control and living empowered lives.

Your turn!

What is something that you can't do because you too are afraid or uncomfortable? It could be anything. The key is to start with something simple and build from there. If you leap into a situation that you aren't ready for and it does not go to plan, it may make you less likely to step outside of your comfort zone in the future.

Some examples:

a. Are you shy or uncomfortable talking to new people?
  - Walk down the street and pay a stranger a compliment, or comment on what a lovely day it is.
  - Hint: Approach someone who does not make you feel intimidated or vulnerable and watch out for body signals. If someone looks like they don't want to be bothered, it's best to direct your attention elsewhere.

b. Do you want to apply for a new job but are terrified of facing an interview?
    - Take steps to prepare for any potential interview. Is there someone you can practise screening questions with? Is it worth consulting a recruitment professional who can assist you with interview techniques and career development?
    - Hint: By eliminating or reducing room for error, you will become more confident in your abilities and will have removed some of the anxieties around the unknown of what 'could' go wrong.

It helps (but is not a necessity) to have a support person on speed dial. When you feel like chickening out, call this person so that they can give you the reinforcement that you can do this!

3. **Dress to impress**

Have you ever heard of the saying 'dress for the job you want, not the job you have'? The way you dress and present yourself can have an incredible impact on your confidence. It affects how other people view you, and more importantly, how you view yourself. You do not have to be the most beautiful person in the room, but if you are walking around with last night's dinner on your shirt and breath that has the potential to kayo the coworker in the cubicle across from you, you should probably start thinking about putting some more effort into your presentation.

Our own presentation can be key to uplifting and empowering ourselves. When we look good, we feel good.

Try getting up just 10 minutes earlier than what you usually would. Use that extra time to pick out a killer outfit, comb your hair and brush your teeth. Apply a dab of lip gloss or a touch of blush if that's what gives you that extra bit of pizazz. Putting in that little bit of extra effort will have you standing proud and poised, ready to take on your day with a fresh feeling of confidence and self-assurance.

Dare to Be Different

'Blue and green should never be seen' was a saying I remember hearing as a child. The combination was garish at best, and offensive at worst. Of course, as time progressed, teaming the colours became quite common. However, just because you can now pair a navy cushion with an emerald throw without repulsing your mother-in-law, doesn't mean that society is void of rules and conventions when it comes to just about everything.

To that I say: dare to be different.

People ought to be free to wear whatever they want. However, how many times have you heard that women can only wear stilettos with a suit, or that men should never let their tie hang below their belt?

Perfection is in the eye of the beholder. Who is to say what is right or what is wrong?

Every Thursday as a child, I would have a sewing lesson

PART 2

with a woman called Mrs Scott. Mrs Scott always wore red lipstick, regardless of the occasion. An opulent brooch – usually decorated with cherries – would embellish the lapels of her stylish tailored suits. In my eyes, Mrs Scott was utterly fabulous.

Mrs Scott had a huge impact in my life. She taught me to always be myself, and to never apologise for it. She made me feel comfortable to express myself, in what I wore and how I acted.

These days, I wear and do whatever I like. Sometimes, I will dress in my most outrageous outfit just to go to the shops. I don't care what people think. I am who I am. For example, every day I wear a flower in my hair. I wear it for my beautiful late mother, because she loved to be out in the garden. Whether I am going to the park, a funeral, or a corporate office, I wear it. I do not care what the occasion is.

Now, not everyone loves the flower as much as I do. I have been told that it is unprofessional and unsuitable. I was in court once and my solicitor told me that the flower was inappropriate! But you know what, that's okay. Not everyone has to like my taste in accessories. What is important is that I know I don't have to change for anybody. I push the boundaries on what I want, when I want, how I want, and you can do that in every part of your life!

When you dare to be different, what you are doing is breaking the mould by operating outside of society's expectations and beliefs. Rather than living within a strict set

PART 2

boundaries, you can create your own rules and opportunities by exploring new ways to complete tasks and achieve goals.

However, daring to be different isn't about doing the opposite of what everyone else is doing. Though technically that would be 'different', there needs to be authenticity in your actions for it to benefit you. Being different requires you to harness and act in accordance with your unique attributes, rather than submitting to external pressures and expectations.

BUT, HOW DOES BEING DIFFERENT BENEFIT ME?

PROFESSIONAL

In a professional setting, when you start thinking outside the box, you will discover innovative ways to implement ideas. By using your natural talents, you will stand apart from the competition and be seen as someone who is creative and forward thinking.

Imagine that you and another colleague are both gunning for the same promotion. You have the same qualifications, the same title, and have worked in the same company for the same amount of time. Who do you think is more likely to get the gig? Joe Blow who meets targets, but has never implemented an original idea in his life? Or you, someone who goes above and beyond to think creatively to execute tasks in fresh and innovative ways?

PART 2

Next time you are asked a question, or faced with a problem to solve at work, brainstorm creative ways of solving it. Could there be a different way to tackle the issue? Is there a fresh perspective that you should consider? You will be surprised at how creative your decision making can be with just a little extra effort!

PERSONAL

Developing meaningful relationships is a key part of the human experience. Our personal relationships define us. They bring us joy and stability. However, it is only when each person is being their true self within the relationship that a successful connection can exist.

Staying true to yourself will not only make you a more interesting person to be around, but will ensure that any relationships that you do have – whether familial, platonic or romantic – will be stronger and more authentic.

Take stock of your relationships. Are you being true to yourself within them? If not, consider why. Perhaps you feel judged by the other person, or that you are not good enough. If you are not being your true self, what purpose does that relationship actually serve?

Life is too short to cling to inauthentic connections. Everyone deserves to be surrounded by people who love them for being their 100% true self, including you!

SPIRITUAL AND POLITICAL

Being brought up Catholic meant that I have never been afraid to explore my spirituality and religiosity. However, as I have gotten older, rather than sticking to rigid religious customs, my focus has shifted to mindfulness practices – like meditation – to connect with the spiritual world.

I have hundreds of crystals that I use in my meditations. There's the Tiger's Eye that's full of asbestos, and the Bumble Bee that carries arsenic in the centre. They are powerful stones that get rid of the bad energies around me.

Connecting with your spirituality grounds you. It does not matter what you believe in, and it is not for anyone else to tell you that your beliefs are wrong. Taking time to reflect on concepts that are bigger than yourself will force you to slow down and take stock of the intangibles that are all around. Practices like meditation and yoga are great ways to de-stress and detoxify the mind and soul.

Like spirituality, it is important to have a strong sense of your political and social beliefs. It is quite common for people to just go with the pack when it comes to socio-political ideals. I refer to these people as 'sheeple'.

Your beliefs should not just bend with the wind. It is important to have a strong sense of what you consider to be right and wrong so that you are able to challenge ideas and actively stand up for what you believe is right. Ask yourself, *what are my core values? What are my expectations from society?* If you see something that does not align with those values, stand up and speak out.

Need some pointers on how to amplify your individuality and become your most daringly different self?

See how I do it below!

1. **Who are you?**

   Before you are truly able to 'dare to be different', you must first have a strong sense of who you are. What are your beliefs and your values? Do you prioritise work, or leisure time? What is it that makes you *uniquely you*?

   For example, I know that I am strong, resilient, hardworking, and outrageous. I value my family above all else. I believe in giving back and helping others. I have a lot of fun and like to make a joke out of most things. I know what I want, so I go out and get it. I never feel ashamed for being myself, or dull my light to pacify others.

   No one is the same as me. So, if I act in line with all the things that make me me, then I am, by default, different. After all, being different really is just *making choices and taking action in accordance with who you are.*

   So, who are *you*?

Write down the first five traits that come to mind if you were to describe yourself to someone else.

1. _____
2. _____
3. _____
4. _____
5. _____

2. Confidence is king

There is no getting around it: being different will require self-confidence. (And I'm not talking about the kind of confidence it takes to wear a flower in your hair.) You will need the sort of confidence that comes with *accepting and loving yourself* – confidence that isn't afraid to yell "I am awesome" and mean it. You will need to trust your gut and love the human being that you are, *more* than you care about what people think or say about you.

I work with many people who have little to none of this. But don't worry, it can be learned! For tips on how to become more confident in your own skin, flick back to the previous chapter.

PART 2

3. **Challenge your thoughts**

From a very young age, we are programmed to think and act in a certain way. We are taught right from wrong, good from bad, how to sit, how to speak, and everything in between. Of course, there is nothing inherently wrong with this. After all, a baby needs to be taught how to do these things by someone!

However, when we are repeatedly given the same speech on what we *should* be doing and how we *should* be doing it, it is inevitable that we will develop ingrained behaviour that can lead to predictable beliefs, ideas and actions. We are set up, almost immediately, with a predetermined path through life, and a manual on how to stick to it.

Have you ever wondered why so many people seem miserable in their daily lives? They have the job, the car, the house, the wife and the kids, but still, they are unhappy. This is because they have followed the manual, rather than listening to their own wants, needs and goals.

To counter this, you must actively think differently. This is harder than it sounds.

Think about whether you *genuinely* like something, or whether you like it just because everyone else does. Perhaps your friends all like chocolate ice cream. That doesn't mean that you have to like chocolate ice cream. Instead, you might like strawberry ice cream. If you like strawberry ice cream instead of chocolate, that's okay. Don't be ashamed, just go out and get a big scoop and enjoy it. It is your life, live it as you choose!

4. **Who surrounds you?**

   Never underestimate the importance of those you surround yourself with. If your circle is actively encouraging and supportive, you will have the drive to be your best authentic self and will feel able to express yourself unreservedly and unashamedly. Your inner circle doesn't have to hold the exact same beliefs that you do, but should give you the space to be yourself without feeling judged or humiliated.

   Do you feel like you are being yourself with those who surround you?

   What changes can you make so that you feel more secure in being yourself within relationships?

5. **Judge away!**

   I hate to be the bearer of bad news, but *people will always judge you and people will always not like you*. Harsh, but true. The silver lining? This means that you have nothing to lose by being yourself!

PART 2

Once you stop caring about what other people think, you will live life more freely, without feeling restricted by others' comments or criticisms. Most of the time, a critic's judgements are just a reflection of their own insecurities anyway, and are not a personal attack on you.

One of my favourite quotes, said by Eunice Camacho Infante, sums it up best:

"In the end, people will judge you anyway, so don't live life impressing others – live life impressing yourself!"

Positivity

I have been told that when I enter a space, I breeze in with so much positivity that everyone can feel it; it's palpable. I learnt this from my mother. Being positive was her way of caring about others. She would often tell me that "you can control the energy and the vibration in a room."

I grew up surrounded by positivity and have always been a very positive person. However, from adolescence right up until my late 20s, there were times when I struggled to remain optimistic. I had many days when I couldn't shake my negativity at all. I developed depression and anxiety and for a long time, just wanted to give up. Eventually, I sought help from a doctor who used medication to get me back on track.

PART 2

I hit my lowest point when I was in recovery in Belgium. The pain was indescribable. I couldn't walk and I could barely talk. I was struggling to stay alive and was only a few steps away from being a complete vegetable. I begged Sal to let me go, but he told me to fight. Those weeks were the toughest of my life; trying to keep myself alive because someone was telling me that they loved me and I couldn't leave them. I was fighting to live every second of every day, even though I desperately wanted to die.

Eventually, the doctors gave me an injection. I had no idea what was in it, but it was the first medication that they had given me that actually made me feel good. With the pain subdued I was able to think more clearly. I realised that I had a choice. I could continue to lay in my misery, *or* I could fight back and change my negative mindset into a positive one.

Once I decided that I was going to actively try and think positively, I eliminated peripheral negative sources. When the nurses offered me a television, I told them, "No, I don't want a TV, I prefer to see what is going on in the real world. I don't want to get focused on sad news stories that the TV will offer me." I became very aware of those around me. If someone was having a bad day, I could sense it immediately.

When doctors or nurses came in and asked, "How are you today?" I would always reply, "Good, how are you?" They could not believe it. My positivity was infectious. "You are always good, Rita."

"Yes," I would say, "because I am alive."

I would always ask, "What's the best thing that's happened to you today?" I loved watching as people reflected on their day to find something positive that happened, despite the challenges they had.

This is one of my blessings – I don't like negativity. I know it is hard not to be negative at times, but you can always find a way of turning a negative into a positive. There is good in everything, you just have to see it. If you are able to live with the reality that good exists, you will be able to see a positive, regardless of your experiences.

GRATITUDE

Being positive is easy when the going is easy. Not so much when the going gets tough.

It is Saturday morning. You wake up and the sun is shining: the weekend is finally here! You have a lovely two days planned – brunch, drinks with the girls, and enjoying some much needed R&R – life is great!

The next 36 hours come and go and before you know it, a dark cloud settles above you. It's Sunday evening. You have to go to work on Monday and the commute is long. You hate your boss and you got caught up in a TV binge session and ran out

PART 2

of time to meal prep. Suddenly, life is not so bright and shiny.

Can any of you relate to this? How would you turn this negative mindset into a positive one?

One of the easiest ways to start seeing the positive, is to remind yourself what it is that you are grateful for. So, you had a fabulous weekend. Why was it so great? Make a list of all the amazing things that contributed to your happiness over those two days. Your friends, the delicious meals, the weather, are all things to be grateful for. The fact that you have a job to go to on Monday is even something to appreciate. Without it, you would not have been able to drop an entire day's pay on all of those cocktails!

If you go into every day with a mentality of gratitude, you will be less likely to experience life as a series of 'doom and glooms', because you have shifted your perspective to focus on the positives.

I recommend starting a gratitude journal, so that when negative thoughts creep in, you can refer to your list. If little things bring a smile to your day, such as the way the sun shines through your kitchen window early in the morning, or the smell of the rain during a storm, add it to the list. When you start taking notice of the small moments, you will surprise yourself as to just how much of your day you appreciate.

Try writing some things below that you are grateful for. If you can't fill in all the lines, consider whether there is something that you have missed. Add more pages if you need. The more you can list, the better!

PART 2

Gratitude Journal

THE RULES ACCORDING TO RITA

PART 2

PRACTICAL WAYS TO STIMULATE POSITIVITY

Do you ever think about the capacity of your brain? It is arguably the most powerful organ in your body and yet, we can get so stuck in an attitude that we are unable to shift our focus. Sometimes, all it takes is something practical, quick and easy to give our brains the shakeup we need.

1. **Move it!**

    Exercise carries with it a string of benefits that promote wellness and positivity. When you move your body, your brain releases chemicals, such as endorphins and serotonin, which can make you feel happier.

    An ancillary benefit of exercise is that it gets you out into the real world. For people who are caught in a negativity spiral, leaving the house can be extremely difficult. By spending just 30 minutes outside exercising, you will notice an immediate positive shift in your overall happiness.

    Exercise can also serve as a distraction, which makes it a great way to de-stress and relieve tension. By focusing on physical activity, rather than your daily troubles, exercise will help you gain clarity, distance and perspective and will take you out of your own head.

2. **Embrace positive people**

   Have you ever spent time talking to an optimistic person and found yourself feeling motivated and uplifted afterward? Or perhaps you have been stuck in a conversation with someone who was exceedingly irritable and complained relentlessly. Did you leave that conversation feeling unmotivated and uninspired? That is no coincidence.

   As we tend to absorb the energy of those around us, it is important to surround yourself with people who motivate, elevate and inspire you. If you are always spending your time with happy people, chances are you will develop a positive outlook on life too. After all, positivity breeds more positivity.

   This isn't to say that you have to ditch every negative person that you know. However, if you are noticing that a certain person or group of people are draining your happy reserves, it may be time to reassess and redefine those relationships.

3. **Do something for someone else**

   As I have mentioned previously in this book, doing a good deed for another person will positively impact on your life, as well as on theirs. Flick back to page 108 for some simple examples of how you can help others.

4. **Do something for *you***

Do things for no other reason than they make you happy. This can be as simple as treating yourself to a decadent bubble bath, or as elaborate as taking yourself on a solo vacation. Make time to treat yourself and you will reap the rewards tenfold.

To Do:
Things that make me happy

☐ _____

☐ _____

☐ _____

☐ _____

☐ _____

☐ _____

☐ _____

☐ _____

HAVE HOPE

At my lowest point, hope was the energy that kept me going. When I finally saw that what had happened to me wasn't my fault, I shifted the blame and released it to the universe. I realised that I still had my undying spirit. I still had my breath, my family and my friends. Witnessing the love, the help and encouragement from my husband, and his undying faith that I would be okay; I decided to live and keep going.

Never underestimate the power of hope. Hope can pull you out of your darkest day and give you the strength to do things you never thought possible. How often do you ever hear someone recover from stage four cancer? Look at me and see the real-life miracle that medical science can be proven wrong. I am a walking billboard for hope in times when there is no hope. If you believe in yourself with hope, everything is possible. Don't give up.

CAN'T GET RID OF THE NEGATIVE?

For some people, no matter how hard they try, the negativity just won't budge. Generally, this is because there is an underlying issue that has affected them that they cannot fix or have not attended to. This type of negativity does not just happen overnight. It takes time.

Nurturing this kind of negativity does not make someone a bad person. It is more likely a result of them not accessing the help that they need. Maybe they don't know where to get help, or perhaps they are in a situation that they cannot control or get out of.

If you are that negative person, I strongly suggest seeking professional help. Speaking to a trained mental health professional will do wonders for your psychological wellbeing. If you are in Australia, your GP can set you up with a Mental Health Care Plan so that you can attend a psychologist at a subsidised rate for a certain number of sessions per year.

If you are dealing with a negative person, the best thing you can do is to simply stay in contact with them. Connect with them every day or every second day. You don't have to talk about the distressing event or topic, but let them know that you are available to talk to. Try to shift the focus onto other subjects, or spend time doing something you both enjoy.[1]

Can you identify some of your own lingering negative feelings? What are some ways you can work on them? Write your answers opposite.

---

1   It is important to remember that you are not your friend/partner/family member's personal therapist. You must maintain boundaries and protect your mental health. There is no point taking on someone else's trauma if it is going to damage your own psychological wellbeing.

THE RULES ACCORDING TO RITA

NEGATIVE THOUGHTS & FEELINGS	STEPS I CAN TAKE

Embrace Life

My late father-in-law Santo and his father Salvatore were extraordinary men who worked hard, day and night, to provide everything their family could ever want. When Santo was finally ready to retire, he built a holiday house in the Southern Highlands and made all the furniture himself. He had built up an empire for his family.

When the house was finally finished, the family hired a truck to bring up all the furniture and slept there overnight for the first time. The following morning, Santo got up to look at the gardens. He had a heart attack and died on the spot. He was only 55 years old. He had never travelled, never been

overseas, never taken the time to slow down and experience life. He was determined to retire at the end of the year so that he could finally relax and enjoy his holiday home, and just like that, his life was cut short before he had a chance to really live.

My mother-in-law, Maria, was a tough woman but she had a good heart. She was born in Australia, but her parents were from Sicily. Maria had a plan to one day travel to Italy with her husband and visit all the places around the world where the most stylish clothes were made. However, the couple always put it off. When he died, Maria said she couldn't go on her own. She was still young at 52, but never remarried. He was the love of her life, so she never moved on, and never went overseas.

PART 2

For years we tried to convince Maria to travel. Occasionally, she would come with us on domestic holidays, but never internationally. She always had an excuse. *Finally*, after assuaging her many concerns, Maria agreed to come on a first-class international holiday with us.

We helped her apply for her ID and visa. We finalised the bookings and insurance. Everything was ready to go. But then, just three months after she got her passport, Maria had a stroke and passed away. She never got to travel outside of Australia.

There are a lot of people who live to an old age, but have never travelled or pampered themselves and have only ever thought about work. It is only once their knees have gone and they can't see straight that they question why they worked so hard to save for retirement in the first place. They have money in the bank but nowhere to spend it, living day by day with feelings of discontent because they could have done so much more with their lives. They live with those regrets until the day they die.

These are learning curves for us all. When you put off the things you want to do until tomorrow, there is a good chance that tomorrow won't come. Don't procrastinate tasks and experiences – we are only guaranteed today. Embrace your life.

Yes, it is important to work hard and set yourself up with a stable future. But, life is not about just that. You have to enjoy the spoils of what that hard work has given you. Take time out to 'smell the roses', because in a flash it can all be gone.

IT'S NOT ABOUT THE MONEY

Often, people tell me that they had a boring weekend and did not do anything. I hate hearing this. I can't help but think, *you have just wasted two days you will never get back!*

A lot of the time, those people blame their financial situation for not going out and having fun. I get it. Life is expensive! If you are scraping to make ends meet, the last thing you want to do is go out and spend money on frivolous activities when there are essentials to be paid for. I *understand* this excuse, but I don't really buy it.

There is an abundance of activities you can do with social groups that are free or do not cost much money and are still good for the soul. Going for a walk or hosting a book club or movie marathon are simple ways that you can have fun with friends or family, without spending a dime. Check whether your local museum or art gallery has a free admission day and plan an outing exploring the exhibitions. If you are willing to spend a little bit of cash, organise a picnic where everyone brings a snack. Once you start getting creative, you will find that there are many fun activities you can enjoy on the weekend, without breaking the bank.

PART 2

CELEBRATE THE SMALL STUFF

Embrace it while you've got it. Every good thing that happens to you, no matter how small or trivial it may seem, is cause for celebration!

Obviously, when something good happens, you feel happy. In fact, the instant that it occurs is the happiest you will feel about it. With every moment that passes, your excitement will dim, until eventually, your exhilaration has been replaced by a fond memory. This is inevitable.

Because of this, it is essential to celebrate each and every small victory, success and happiness to the fullest. You only get one shot, before that moment starts to pass you by.

Your job (at long last) gives you a pay rise? Go ballistic! Your partner finally stops leaving wet towels on the bed after your months of gentle nagging? Sing from the rooftops! Don't let that moment be robbed from you, because tomorrow that level of excitement won't be there. Once it has passed, you will never have the opportunity to celebrate in quite the same way.

I remember when I turned 30. It was a massive milestone! I had been given the 'eight months to live' sentence in my 20s, and yet there I was in my third decade still standing. So, you can imagine how extraordinary this birthday was for me and my family.

To celebrate, I threw a huge party and invited 150 people to my home. My birthday cake was a towering croquembouche, made up of hundreds of profiteroles filled with chocolate and vanilla custard, with layers of toffee coating the outside. It was completely over the top, but I made it happen. I needed to celebrate my life up to that point with an event like no other.

Then, for my 50th birthday, I designed a decadent five-tiered cake. I put so much thought, time and effort into creating it, with each layer representing a decade of my life. It was covered in decorations – diamantes, pink leopard print, rosary beads, a magic hat with cards and dice, a princess crown, and exquisite long feathers. Everyone could see that that cake was a symbol of my life. It played such a big part in my special day.

When you do it, do it to the fullest. Let the fireworks go off and celebrate each win as often as you can. Hold onto every success and revel in your happiness for as long and as passionately as you can.

LIVE IN THE NOW!

My life is like a cookbook. I turn a page, see a recipe, and decide what I will cook that day. I take each day as it comes.

My health challenges have constantly reminded me how fleeting this life is. I truly acknowledge the magical moments that exist inside every day – the moments that are often missed if you don't take the time to look for them. I choose to live in the present, rather than worrying about the past and being depressed with regret about things that have already happened and that I cannot change. I try not to stress about a future that may or may not come.

Living in the now is accepting what happened yesterday, and not worrying about what is going to happen tomorrow. It involves taking action and doing what you want in every moment of every day. To live in the moment is to live presently and mindfully – observing and engaging fully with the world that surrounds you.

You have the choice to live for today and go out and do the things that you want to do, when you want to do them. Right now, you could get in the car and drive wherever you like. You could eat whatever you want, or talk to whomever you wish.

Live in the now, but how?
If simple experiences are taken away from you, it becomes significantly more difficult to live in the moment. There were times when I was so sick that I could not do anything except lay in bed. During these periods, I was definitely not living in the 'now'. I was dying. While my body was dwindling away to a skeleton, my mind became centred around fear, apprehension, and regret.

When you have no control over your life, it is easy for your mindset to become one of worry, rather than one of acceptance and living in the moment. This makes sense. If you are not satisfied with your situation, why would you want to remain present there? Of course your mind is going to wander and start catastrophising about the future. You may also start romanticising the past as a form of escapism from your present reality. When I was sick, this was how I lived, until one day I decided to do something about it.

First, I stopped complaining and feeling sorry for myself. There was no point in saying "Why me?" or "How could this have happened?" It was just not good enough. I realised that I had to get up and take full responsibility for my own life. I had to play the hand I was dealt – there was no point agonising over things that had already happened that I could not control.

Then, I ingrained a (perhaps grim, given my health status) sentiment into my psyche:

> *Don't worry about tomorrow, because who knows if you are going to wake up tomorrow. You have to worry about today, for today.*

Whenever I started worrying about what could happen, I repeated the mantra. I constantly reminded myself that I could not fix what happened yesterday, just like I could not change what comes tomorrow.

Once I learned how to control my anxious thoughts, I was able to live more peacefully. Even on my darkest days I learnt to mute my fearful mind. Even if you think that you cannot do it, just try. If it does not work the first time, try again. The brain is like a powerful machine. If I was able to do it, so can you.

Another handy tip is to look back on something that you were stressed about in the past. Are you still stressed about it now? Chances are, you aren't. You are more likely to look back on that past stress and think something like, *wow, I lost a lot of sleep worrying about that. Why was I so strung out?* Reminding yourself that it all worked out last time will help you overcome present stresses and act more rationally.

Appreciation

It is usually the people we assume will always be there, and the things we expect to happen every day, that we don't fully appreciate. We don't acknowledge our loved ones enough because we have never imagined life without them. We don't turn our minds to the privilege of being able to accomplish simple tasks, because we would never anticipate that these things could be taken away from us. Often, it is only once we lose something that we truly acknowledge its value.

After my operation in Belgium, I could not walk or talk. The ability to place one foot in front of the other, or string a simple sentence together, were two things that I never imagined would be taken from me. Though I had been aware that walking and talking were dexterities that I very much relied on, I had never taken the time to step back and truly recognise my privilege in using those functions every day.

Throughout the process of relearning those basic skills, I came to truly understand just how valuable they were to me. From then on, I vowed to appreciate everything in my life, and to not wait until it was taken away before doing so.

Now, I appreciate everything and everyone that I have in my life. There is nothing that I take for granted. From the time I rise in the morning, to when I go to bed at night, I acknowledge each small part of my day that, together, shapes my whole life.

Think about the miracle that human life is, and that you get to experience it. When you wake up in the morning, do you have the ability to walk to your window and open the blinds? Do you have access to running water and food in the fridge? When you come home after a long day of work, do you enjoy the luxury of sitting on the couch and relaxing in front of the television? These are all things to be appreciative of. The fact that you can walk, that there is a roof over your head, that you can access amenities like water and electricity, that you have a job to go to, are all things to be grateful for. Think about the fact that you woke up at all. That, in and of itself, is something to cherish.

GIVE APPRECIATION AND THANKS

Life is what you make it. Some days I am in the shop unpacking boxes, lifting heavy items and stocking shelves, cleaning or dusting. Other days I am sipping champagne with the best of the best, dining in nice restaurants and attending glamorous events. No matter where I am or what I am doing, I always make sure to acknowledge and give thanks to those who surround me.

STRANGERS

How many times a day do other people help us out? When you think about it, lots! Whether it is a commuter giving up their seat on the train, or a waiter grabbing a bowl of water for your dog at the café, strangers regularly offer us a helping hand for no other reason than to make our lives that little bit more comfortable.

It should go without saying that whenever someone does something for you, you must say thank you and *mean it*. It really doesn't cost anything to merely acknowledge people who are making your environment a happier place. There are times when I walk into public toilets and there are cleaners working. I always thank them. A little love goes a long way.

Acknowledging others has a ripple effect. Thanking someone who does a good deed will not only make them feel appreciated in that moment, but will encourage them to continue assisting others (AKA will provide positive reinforcement). Imagine if every time someone held a door open, or let someone cut in the coffee line, they were ignored or treated rudely. They would probably stop making an effort in this way. Be sure to thank people who go the extra mile so that they keep acting positively. Also, if bystanders see a good deed being done and appreciated, they will be more likely to start helping people themselves.

Next time a stranger does something for you, remember to thank them. Other simple ways you can show acknowledgement include tipping wait staff for good service, cleaning up after yourself at a restaurant, or writing a good review for a business. It doesn't have to take much effort or cost much money. A simple gesture of acknowledgement can make a world of difference to someone.

FAMILY AND FRIENDS

The thing that I am most grateful for is my family. There are so many people out there who do not have one. I can pick up the phone and talk to my family at any time of the day or night. I do not take that for granted.

We often assume that our family and friends know how valued they are, so we neglect showing them the appreciation they deserve. We come to *expect* their generosity and kindness, when we should be actively expressing our gratitude. It is important to make our loved ones feel loved so that they know they are not taken for granted.

Showing meaningful appreciation for loved ones should be easy. After all, you already know their personality, their likes and their dislikes. Giving thanks can be much more personal, as you can tailor the way that you show appreciation for your relationship. Taking a loved one out for dinner, sending a personalised gift, or displaying physical affection are easy ways to show that you are grateful for their companionship. Sending a handwritten thank you note or composing a heartfelt letter are also great ways to communicate sincere thanks.

However, when it comes to friends and family, it is more about consistency than 'one-off' gestures when it comes to making the other person feel appreciated. Reliably supporting your loved ones' goals, keeping in regular and positive contact, and making yourself available to provide emotional support will usually mean more than sporadic displays of gratitude. Show your appreciation by letting your loved ones know that their mere existence is valued and that you recognise the joy they bring to your life.

GIVE BACK

I love to travel. It is something that is very valuable to me so

I try to do it whenever I can. However, I appreciate that not everyone has the ability or opportunity to do this. I know some people who have never even been on a holiday.

I truly appreciate the privilege I have in being able to jet off across the globe, and I will never take that for granted. So, whenever I go overseas, I always dedicate at least one day to charity work. This makes me feel as though I am giving back, and that my holiday was worthwhile and not just about me.

In 2014, Sal and I celebrated our twenty-fifth wedding anniversary by renewing our vows in Phuket. Our friends and family all travelled to Thailand for the occasion and spent three weeks with us. It was perfect.

I designed a stunning pink gown, which I had custom made to wear for the ceremony. The top of the dress was dazzling, made from a fitted corset encrusted with silver and pink beads. Pink ruffles gathered at the waist, which stretched into an 8.2 metre train constructed of soft silk flowers, lace, and tulle. It ended up being longer than Princess Diana's wedding dress!

We had three celebrations that spanned over the course of a week. More than 100,000 fresh flowers in pink, white and purple embellished each event. Grand arches filled with blooms framed us as we said our promises to one another. It was my perfect romantic fairy tale. It was so magical that we appeared in multiple newspaper articles and magazines all over the world.

THE RULES ACCORDING TO RITA

After the celebrations wound up, we personally delivered the leftover flowers to the local hospitals and nursing homes. It was Mothers' Day week and we wanted to spread love and joy to the residents within the community.

Instead of asking for gifts, Sal and I requested that our guests make donations to our wishing well, which would be spent on supplies for the local Phuket orphanages. Each children's home gave us a list of items to buy that would help them out. We travelled to the supermarket and the meat market and purchased everything we could to make a difference for that week. With the remainder of the money, we bought gifts for the hotel staff who looked after us like rock stars.

I dedicate a lot of time to charity work. In 2020 I was awarded a Cook Community Award from Prime Minister Scott Morrison for my valued contribution to the public. Giving back is something I have always done – it keeps me grounded. If there is something I can donate that will help someone, whether it be my time, money, or objects, I will do my absolute best to facilitate that contribution. Giving back and helping others is one of the ways that I show my appreciation for what I have.

Creativity

I have always been extremely creative and hands on. When I was a little kid, if I couldn't buy something, I would make it. I remember not being able to afford high-heels as a teenager and building a pair of wedges out of a wood block and my mother's material.

Growing up, I was determined to feed my creativity. I excelled at art and eventually discovered a passion for music, particularly piano and guitar. I taught myself as much as I could, but I desperately wanted to attend professional lessons to refine my skills.

I begged my dad to let me take classes. Unfortunately, but unsurprisingly, a resounding "no" was his only answer. For weeks, I pleaded with him to let me go, but he would not budge. His decision was resolute.

His mind may have been made up, but so was mine. Determined to nurture my passion, I booked a guitar lesson behind dad's back. I scheduled it for a Saturday morning – market day – in the hope that I could sneak off without him knowing. I knew that he would be down in Sydney at Flemington for the day, so it was the perfect opportunity to squeeze in a class. Dad would be none the wiser.

I went to the lesson and loved every second of it. It was like a fire had been ignited within me – I craved to learn more. Finally, I was doing something to satiate my appetite for creativity. I was doing something just for *me*.

As thrilled as I was, Dad was just as furious. Despite my crafty planning, he found out that I had disobeyed him, and when I got home I copped a belting. But that did not stop me. Every week I went to my lesson and every week I would be in trouble.

On and on this went, until eventually, Dad started to embrace my learning music. It took an entire year, but he finally realised how important the lessons were to me. From then on, he let me go without so much as a raised eyebrow. Eventually, he grew to not just tolerate, but to *enjoy* my playing. He also let my sister learn the piano, and the two of us would practise together while Dad stared back in admiration.

From then on, I have poured as much time and energy as possible into my creative endeavours. When I am not creative I am not happy, because I am not being true to myself.

When I got sick, my depression escalated because the creative side of me became forcefully dormant. I didn't have the energy to work, so I didn't have the energy to play. Even though my mind was sharp, my body was weak and fragile.

Gradually, I was able to pick up a pen and paper and started designing bits and pieces on A4 sheets, drawing and crafting little toys. I would read books, watch videos – anything that could stimulate the imaginative side of me. I started making games and taught myself how to face paint, practising on a piece of plastic and then wiping it off. Sal would go out and buy me the paints and cardboard to work with. My daily focus was on my creative mind to get me through the day.

There were only about two or three hours a day I spent creating, but at least I was doing something productive rather than feeling sorry for myself. Laying around watching television got me down, but being creative energised me. If I didn't complete what I was doing one day, I would look forward to getting up the next to finish it.

It was during this time that Barbee Barb Children's Entertainment was born. There were many days spent in bed, but I was always creating. I worked as much as possible. The birthing of my business kept me alive. It was like watering a seed, nurturing it every day and watching it grow. It gave me a sense of purpose.

I still suffer side effects that make it hard for me to get a word out or articulate a sentence. There are days I slur my speech because I am overtired or my medications haven't kicked in properly. On those days, the best thing to do is just calm down, stay in, and get creative.

Your turn!

If there is a topic or area that inspires you, think of ways that you can get creative with it. It doesn't have to be something that takes up a lot of your energy. Play around and see what works for you.

If you are lost with where to start, draw inspiration from stimulus around you. Pull out a magazine or book about a topic that you are interested in. Once you begin reading, you will feel more motivated to take a stab at commencing your own creative project. For example, if you are reading a book on painting, think about how you would make your own art. If you are flicking through a gardening magazine, use the inspiration to start planning your own outdoor sanctuary. Surrounding yourself with things that stimulate your creative mind will encourage you to get out there and give it a go.

Once you have found your creative outlet, try practising it for just a short time every day. Instead of watching that extra episode of trashy television, get up and put your mind to work. Try setting aside just half an hour each evening to create something that is just for you.

What are some creative projects you just can't wait to try? List them here!

_____

_____

_____

_____

_____

_____

Optimise Opportunities

Because Barbee Barb was created while I was sick, my goals and considerations were different to that of the ordinary small business owner. Being sick meant that I had to create my own opportunities: it wasn't as if I could go out and spruik my services to the world from the confines of my bed. I had to get creative by devising how I could best promote my business, while still supporting my health needs. What were my goals and expectations? What were my limits?

Once I defined my goals and limits and started working with them in mind, I was able to maximise my time, productivity and energy. I learnt how to create, tailor, and elevate opportunities so that they were beneficial to my business, while still catering to my health needs. By having a clear direction of what I wanted and how I was going to achieve it, I was able to successfully balance my competing interests and advance my career.

When Barbee Barb Children's Entertainment first got off the ground, I was undergoing cancer treatment (radiotherapy, chemotherapy and laser therapy) while performing live as Barbie at children's birthday parties. This was extremely tough on my body. However, because I had already considered and factored my health restraints into the job, it somehow worked. My success was not obstructed by my illness.

I made sure that my treatments were administered on a Tuesday or Wednesday. That way, I could sleep through Monday and Thursday and still have all day Friday to prepare for my weekend shows. It was not ideal, but I had found a way to do what I loved, while also managing my illnesses. The weeks flew by. It was chaotic, but I had a routine.

Too often, I hear people say that they can't do what they want to do because it is not the right time – they need more money, they can't leave their job yet, their kids are too young.

They put off their goals waiting for the 'perfect' moment. News flash: that moment will never come. There will always be something 'more important' and something 'more pressing' that will stand in between those people and their goals. The truth is, they are too afraid to turn their dreams into reality, so they hide behind excuses.

Where there is a will, there's a way. It will require hard work, but by acknowledging your limitations and creating a plan that works around them, you will be more likely to reach your goals. How can you create and optimise opportunities that work for you? Think about it and make it happen!

KEY RELATIONSHIPS

Depending on your goals, it is unlikely that you will be able to fully optimise opportunities on your own. Chances are, you will need guidance from experienced individuals who can help you leverage your skills and point you in the right direction.

Networking is a great way to get a head start on your goals. By reaching out to people who have knowledge in the area that you want to get involved with or progress in, you will gain access to invaluable help and information. The more people you connect with, the more comprehensive and far-reaching the advice will be. Even if you think you know what you are doing, there will always be a benefit to seeking as much guidance as you can. All it takes is one conversation to get the ball rolling.

Not every person that you meet will be able to set you up with an opportunity straight away. However, this does not mean that the connection is no longer of benefit to you. Chances are that if you have made a good impression on that person, they will introduce you to people within their own network who may be able to give you a leg up or offer advice.

If you don't know where to start, try reaching out to someone who you admire and ask them to meet up for a coffee. If they are too busy, suggest scheduling a phone call. It may seem intimidating at first, but the more you put yourself out there, the more confident you will become. After all, if someone is passionate about what they do, chances are that they will be more than happy to discuss it with you. They will appreciate that you have taken an interest in their journey in an area of mutual interest.

LIFE IS WHAT YOU MAKE IT

As human beings, we are not perfect. We are each inherently flawed and unique and exceptional. We are not the same, even though we may have similar limbs and organs.

We are all dealt a plate when we enter this world. We are born into a set of circumstances that we have no control over. We cannot choose who our parents are, where we live, or what we are named. Many decisions are made for us that we have no input into or involvement with.

PART 2

However, as we grow, we are given more autonomy to change what is on our plate. We are given a set of tools that we can use to develop and alter our life trajectory.

There is no point in blaming your present situation on your past circumstances. There is an opportunity every day to change something that you don't like about your life. Every decision you make impacts your future self, and if you want to, you can change your fate. That is up to you.

I have done it. I was dealt a plate, and I have changed countless things that were served on that plate. I came from a family of immigrant farmers. I grew up working on the land and developed a severe illness as a teenager that killed me (not once, but twice)! No matter how many times I was told "no," no matter how many times my body failed me, no matter how many times they said that I would never be able to walk or talk again, I persevered and succeeded in achieving my dreams. I created my own destiny.

It really comes down to you. Your perseverance and strength will determine whether or not you can reinvent yourself and change your fate. If you are not changing something, then you are choosing it. This is not easy, but can be done if you are focused and can adapt to change.

Start by thinking about what it is that you would like to change in your life. Is it something small that may just take a few weeks to solve, or is it a 'big picture' adjustment that will require strategy and planning? Focus on exactly what it is that you are unhappy with and write it below.

> What do I want to change?

_____

_____

_____

> Next, think about what you would need to do to solve the problem by clearly articulating what your goal is. For example, if the problem is that you hate your job, your goal might be quitting to find a new one.
>
> What can I do to make this change?

_____

_____

_____

PART 2

Now it is time to map out a plan as to how you could go about achieving that goal. Using the above example, the steps you would need to take would be: updating your resume, searching and applying for jobs, practising interview techniques (so on and so forth).

What steps do I need to take to achieve my goal?

_____

_____

_____

_____

The last, and most crucial step, is to execute the plan. Each time you complete one small step, you will be that tiny bit closer to achieving your end goal. By breaking your goal down into manageable tasks, you will feel less overwhelmed and more accomplished.

{ Reflect on how you executed your plan. Are there any other steps you should be taking?

_____

_____

_____

_____

Rita is sharing more in her INTERACTIVE book.

See exclusive downloads, videos, audios and photos.

DOWNLOAD it now at
www.deanpublishing.com/magicandmiracles

Courage

When my 17-year-old father decided he must escape Italy, he had no idea where that journey would take him. It wasn't until two years later – when two ships destined for two different countries rolled into the harbour – that he found himself at the crossroads: France, or Australia?

On one hand, he could jump on the ship to France. The distance was shorter – being just a three-week journey. Alternatively, he could embark on the arduous three-month voyage across the sea to the land down under.

As the boarding line split between destinations, most of those queuing veered toward the French vessel. My dad did not follow. His stomach told him that despite his fear – of the unknown, of the journey, and of what was waiting for him on the other side of the world – that in order to start a better life, he had to get on the boat *Castel Blanco*, the boat to Australia.

Because of my dad's courage and strength, I was given the opportunity to grow up in a privileged country surrounded by loving family and friends. We worked hard, but we never struggled for food, housing or education. We were always safe and healthy.

I am eternally grateful to have inherited my father's fearlessness. Without it, I would not have made it through those many years of illness and pain, let alone have forged the beautiful life that I now live.

You wouldn't believe it, but deep down, I am a shy person. Growing up, I never shared my space with anyone. I was especially prudent when it came to exposing my body and hated getting changed in front of other people. Now, I am a confident and outgoing person. If something frightens me, I try my best to find the courage to overcome my reservations and complete the task.

Over the years, I have become comfortable in my own

skin, and am not as reserved as I once was. After being exposed physically and handled by so many people while I was sick, my inhibitions dissipated. I realised how insignificant it was to be worried about what other people saw and thought of me, and became more relaxed and assertive. I learnt to be courageous and strong.

It's funny, my shyness seemed to have been cured by illness.

NO FEAR

Fear is a natural emotion that we have developed as part of our survival skills. It is instinctive and is our body's way of reacting to danger by alerting us that we should escape a threatening situation to find security. Everyone experiences fear at some point in their lives.

Fear is not always a bad thing. You know the feeling you get when you look over the edge of a cliff? Or the apprehension you have when driving through rough weather? Those are feelings of fear. Your instincts are protecting you from something dangerous (perhaps falling to your death or swerving into oncoming traffic). That is good fear.

Bad fear exists when there is no real danger to be frightened of – the scary outcome exists only in the mind. This type of fear can be so powerful, that even though there may be no real prospect of it occurring, it can still influence our decision-making and stop us from doing the things we want to do. Over time, people who are governed by this type of fear may limit their happiness, opportunities, and successes. For some, this type of fear can be almost debilitating.

So, how can it be overcome?

1. **Practice makes perfect**

    It may sound obvious, but the more we do something, the less frightening it becomes. Regularly practising the things that we are nervous about gives us the opportunity to see that the outcomes are not as bad or as scary as we projected in our minds. Through repetition, we can gain confidence in our abilities to work through the situation or problem.

2. **Forgive yourself**

    Sometimes, fear can build up as a result of putting too much pressure on ourselves. When we don't perform perfectly, or if something does not go exactly to plan, we are left feeling like failures. We beat ourselves up about what we did not do and what we should have done. This can breed fear for our future selves, as we let one 'imperfect' experience influence our mindset when entering similar situations.

    For me, I am extremely hard on myself. I want to be the best I can be in everything that I do. I do not like it when I give a sub-par performance, or something does not turn out the way that I had planned. If I make a mistake, I have a tough time reconciling it in my mind and accepting the blunder.

However, over the years, I have learnt that this is not a productive or useful way to react. I have come to accept that if I make an error, the best thing to do is to forgive myself and move on, which is perhaps easier said than done.

Recently, I threw a book launch for about 150 people. On the night, I had planned a little surprise for my guests. I prepared a speech that I would deliver before launching into song and dance. In the lead up to the event, I rehearsed religiously. The entire performance was polished to a tee.

Everything was going according to plan. I waltzed onto the stage in my sparkly red dress, ready to begin my presentation. All eyes were on me. Then suddenly, the music sped up. The introduction of the song started to play before I had even begun my speech!

I was thrown completely off balance. I could either stop the music and continue with my speech as planned, *or* I could launch straight into verse one. Without time to think, I started singing.

I performed the piece well, and after it finished, received a huge round of applause. The audience loved it. They were none the wiser that an entire section of the show had been missed.

However, despite their overwhelming support, I could

not help but feel that I had let myself down. The performance I gave was not the one I wanted to give. There was so much that I did not get to say by omitting my speech.

The overwhelming feelings of failure, of being imperfect, sidled into my mind. I was frustrated with myself – unhappy and dissatisfied. *Why did that have to happen? Why wasn't it perfect like I had rehearsed?*

I took a few deep breaths and tried to shake it off. I told myself what I already knew: I could not change what had already happened. I had done my best, and in any event, the audience loved what I did. It was hard, but eventually I was able to congratulate myself, move on, and enjoy the rest of the night.

We are not perfect, ever. While it is important to plan for variables, we cannot allow ourselves to get caught up in over-preparing. When we do this, it becomes harder for us to cope when things do not stick exactly to the script. We must learn to take experiences as they come, and let go of them once they happen. If something does not work out, we have to be kind to ourselves, forgive, and move on.

Because I successfully moved on from that experience, I was able to get back on that stage and perform without any additional pressure or fear. Every time I get up in front of an audience to talk, sing, or dance in the future, my previous experience will not negatively impact my frame of mind.

3. **Distraction**

   Sometimes, it is hard to shift the fear from your mind. Even with years of practice, I still struggle to overcome my nerves and anxieties, but find a way to move forward at a steady pace that suits me.

   I have found that distracting myself is a great way to get on with my day, when I cannot stop focusing on my fears and worries.

   Find something that you enjoy and makes you happy. This can be anything – from zoning out to the television to baking a cake. If spending time by yourself just creates a hotbed of overthinking and under-relaxing, try spending some time exercising outside or catching up with friends. Focusing on tasks that you enjoy will not only provide a short term distraction from your worries, but will leave you feeling happier and more calm for the rest of the day.

4. **Meditation**

   Through meditation, I have been able to relieve my stresses and anxieties as they arise. If I ever feel fearful or apprehensive, a simple relaxation exercise will calm my nerves and ground me back in reality.

   The benefits of meditation are far-reaching. Meditation is not just useful 'in the moment', but also promotes a calm and peaceful mindset day to day. With consistent practice, meditation can leave you feeling more able to face high-stress situations without becoming overwhelmed or anxious. Regular meditation can bring inner harmony to daily life.

Perhaps the opposite to distraction, meditation involves spending time alone grounding yourself. It is an internal activity to *focus* the mind, rather than distraction which uses external stimuli to *occupy* the mind.

There are many different ways to meditate. A quick google will explain the various techniques of meditation and their benefits. At the end of the day, no particular method is right or wrong. It is purely a matter for you to discover what works best for you.

I have found that grounding myself with Mother Nature is crucial to my meditation, and I recommend it to all who want to dabble in the practice.

How to meditate:
Go outside and stand on the grass barefoot. Concentrate on the feeling of the ground beneath your toes as the earth absorbs the tension and static that has built up in your body. You can ground yourself on any natural surface, whether it be grass, soil or sand.

Next, lay down on the ground and try entering a meditative state. This will assist your body in attracting energy from

} Mother Earth. This connection with nature will stimulate a clear mind and draw out other negative energies.

FAKE IT 'TIL YOU MAKE IT!

A common misconception is that everyone has their life together more than you do. Take your best friend: she gets up at 5:30 am for the gym, is in the office before 8 am *and* somehow manages to drink two litres of water a day. Then you have your co-worker who balances a bigger client list than you but still finds the time to cook restaurant-quality meals for her kids and hubby every night. On the other hand, you struggle to drag yourself to the shower before the latest train gets in and your idea of a home-cooked meal is a microwave lasagne followed by a bag of cheese rings. Everyone you look at seems to be more organised, more happy, and more financially stable than you. How?

Because, at some point in life, everybody has faked it for the outside world.

But, this isn't necessarily a bad thing ...

Sometimes, we need to overplay our abilities so that we have the courage to achieve goals and get where we want to be. For example, *acting* like you are confident in a job interview will make you *look* like a confident person. The interviewer does not know that you are actually sweating bullets beneath your blazer, nor do they need to. You have presented a version of yourself that is self-assured, level-headed and reacts well under pressure.

This follows the idea that to be able to learn some skills and behaviours, we first must act like we have them. With enough practice, this 'fake' behaviour will become natural. Essentially, you are just learning how to do something, by doing it!

Don't ever let a lack of confidence stop you from going for your goals. Everyone starts somewhere, and there is nothing wrong with fudging it a bit along the way.

Just remember, you never truly know someone's journey or how they view themselves internally. Someone who looks 'together' might consider themselves to be a bigger mess than you! Be kind to yourself, and try not to compare yourself to others. Stay true to who you are and what you are capable of sustaining.

Kindness

No matter who you are or what you do, kindness should be the epicentre of your existence. In a world so full of negativity and hate, being kind is something we can each do to make life a better experience for everyone.

If you are only going to practise one thing in this book, make it kindness and respect. Being kind is the easiest, yet most important action you can take. It does not take much to simply act with care and compassion.

DON'T JUDGE A BOOK BY ITS COVER
Remember playing in the schoolyard and there would always

be that one boy who picked on any kid smaller than him? Or that group of girls whose sole mission was to make everyone's life around them a living hell? People often assume that once you graduate from times tables and lunches in brown paper bags, that bullying automatically disappears. Unfortunately, this is not the case. Bullying can occur at any point in a person's life, whether they are 6, 16, or 60. Bullying is indiscriminate.

As soon as I enter a room, there are eyes on me. I am judged the minute I walk in. Sometimes, I can just about hear the whispers and sniggers going on behind my back.

This is never a nice feeling. Being who I am – with all my glitz and glamour – is always bound to cause a stir. I have a presence about me that makes people either love me or hate me. I am used to it.

Over the years, I have learnt how to grow a thick skin and brush the bullies off. By loving who I am, and staying true to that person, I have enough confidence to not let what other people think affect me. I decided a long time ago that I was not going to change for anybody. If someone does not like me, then that is just too bad. I say, "Move on!"

However, not everyone is able to build an impenetrable wall of confidence around their feelings. Just one hurtful comment can derail someone's day, and a series of targeted attacks has the potential to ruin an entire life. You never know what someone else is going through until you have walked a mile in their shoes.

That is why we must always be kind to one another. If someone is different to you, celebrate it! If you don't agree with the way someone lives their life, respect their choice and leave them be. We are all in this life together. We must support and uplift one another as much as we can.

TO MY FRIEND, BARRY COLLINS

How many social media profiles do you see that are littered with photos boasting beautiful stories and interesting lives? These pages have thousands of 'followers' – people who like the pictures but are no more than faces behind a screen.

I know many people who have experienced significant personal setbacks – family breakups, divorce, mental illness – yet you would never pick this from the newsfeed. Online their lives look flawless; each picture a billboard of picturesque travels, delicious meals, and a bustling social life. Their pictures make it look as if nothing ever goes wrong, that every day is bright and wonderful.

But that is no more than a highlight reel showcasing a few carefully curated snapshots that have been manipulated to look like everyday life. It is just an outlet. It is not a true and honest representation of what someone is going through day to day. We create an image that is not real. My late friend was a perfect example of this.

Barry and I were great friends. We would catch up on daily

life. He would always pop into my shop, just to chat the hours away. For two hours he would travel, just to give me a bunch of flowers and some custard rhubarb tarts. Sometimes, he would hang out in my office all day.

Barry was a cameraman, and at one stage had worked as a security guard for one of Australia's most famous prime ministers. He knew everyone and was the go-to guy for all things audiovisual. Whether it was a fashion shoot, a makeup commercial, or a store opening, Barry was always the first to offer up his services and lend a helping hand. He was extremely generous.

What drew me to Barry was his endless positivity. He was always telling me how good life was. He constantly acted like he had something on or somewhere to be. If I ever needed a hand with something, Barry always had a friend who knew a bloke who could help me out. To the outside world, Barry seemed to be living a perfectly happy life. I had assumed he had a lot of friends.

One day, Barry posted a photo on Facebook. It was of a forest on a cold winter's morning. The photo was stunning – a foggy scene of dark trees, interrupted only by fragments of yellow light. The post had hundreds of likes, mostly from his friends and followers, of which his social media page had thousands.

Twenty minutes after posting the picture, Barry had a heart attack while out walking alone. Somehow, someone eventually found him and he was rushed to hospital. The police got his phone and went through it in search of a regular contact. I, surprisingly, was the main caller and receiver.

Once police got hold of me and explained what had happened, I put out an urgent message on Barry's Facebook page, asking if anyone nearby could go to his bedside. I was two hours away, so I could not get there immediately. I did not get a response.

Barry was on life support for three days until he was pronounced brain dead. To my disbelief, the only person by his bedside was me.

Even though I reached out on his Facebook page, to his thousands of 'friends' and followers, no one cared. When Barry needed support most, he had no one. I could not believe it. It was devastating.

There is a lot of loneliness in this world. Just because someone looks happy on the outside, or like they have a lot of friends, doesn't necessarily mean that they are or that they do. After all, Barry had one million followers on social media. On his deathbed, he had no one.

Don't assume that everyone has a support network to lean on. Check in regularly with your friends and family, especially those that you haven't heard from in a while. A lot of the time, if someone is in need, they won't feel able to reach out. It is up to you to make that first move. It is your responsibility to make your loved ones feel loved.

THE RULES ACCORDING TO RITA

Rita's Parting Philosophy

The Future is Thrust Upon Me

When I died on the operating table in Belgium in the early 1990s, some crazy things happened to me. Okay, I mentioned that I woke up haemorrhaging heavily on the bed, I also did not know who I was, where I came from or what had happened to me. I had to regain my memories, and learn to talk and walk from the beginning, again. I often reminisce of my time in the bright fields of flowers or floating over my hospital bed, watching my "dead" body.

My mind felt scrambled between my new reality, learning my past and relationships, and the euphoria of my journey to Heaven. During the ensuing years, I noticed that I had "feelings" and premonitions, not constantly, but sporadically, when least expected. Certain people and events tended to trigger me, to have feelings about those people or events, to show me outcomes about them that were not predictable. It seemed that I was experiencing psychic flashes. However, I felt vulnerable; I felt that if I told them what I felt or saw, that they would think I was crazy, due to my many lengthy medical events and numerous medications. Thus, I only told these thoughts to my husband, and one of my sisters. Initially, these feelings were quite rare, but over the years, their frequency multiplied manyfold. I was so embarrassed, as my husband scoffed at them for years, and my sister thought it was interesting, but began to believe in their legitimacy as they became more frequent and accurate. Even my husband, the sceptic, acknowledged and understood my newfound abilities years later, as we watched TV shows about celebrity mediums, such as John Edwards, Allison DuBois, Tyler Henry and Theresa Caputo.

In the meantime, I had enrolled in a public speaking course, with The Speakers' Institute, and attended and subsequently completed the course. This course forced and encouraged me to finally open up about my medical history, medications, operations and death. Confronting my past and opening up about this was a difficult journey as I had never told anyone else. My husband knew, of course, and tried to encourage me to be more open. However, I had thought that if anyone knew about it all, they would either feel sorry for me, because I could not have children, or would see me as defective or disabled. I did not want to be perceived as weak. So being forced to tell my story on stage, in front of my class, over and over again, inspired a confidence in my own strength and abilities, so that I was able to write my first book, about my medical journey, and this subsequent book of my memoirs.

Being a farm girl, I am used to doing everything for myself. I do my own hair, nails and waxing. I do not believe in shortcuts to beauty treatments, so I only use the best products, and do my own research for the most suitable products. But my flaw is that I am a perfectionist, and very hard to please. I concluded that as good as my cosmetics are, they still fell short of my expectations, and I knew I could do better. I felt I had to design my own range of cosmetics, in order to improve the results of each item.

- Lipsticks
- Rouges
- Foundations
- Eyeliners
- Eyeshadows
- Skin moisturisers
- And more …

Checkout my website www.thered-peacock.com

RITA'S PARTING PHILOSOPHY

I was invited to join the Steering Committee for HerStory Women's Global Empowerment and to travel to 248 destinations around the world, delivering and convening these conferences. So, we started with Las Vegas, USA in July 2019, then went through Europe, starting with Germany and Poland. This was followed by a New Zealand Conference during the planning of the Conference I was organising in Sydney, and only a week prior. Sydney in December 2019 was the first that I planned alone and organised from scratch. And what a success! Then, shortly after came the big lockdown. The Canadian Conference in Edmonton where I was to be the headline speaker had to be cancelled, as were dozens of others worldwide.

While we were locked down during COVID-19, my new "powers" came to the fore, as I was forced to stay isolated at home, so I would not catch COVID in the community. COVID-19 was spreading so rapidly that I feared for my safety, because of my compromised immune system, so I had no desire to mix with the community; not even with friends or family. Being isolated at home seemed to sharpen my abilities. It soon became evident that I was actually channelling, and that I was even able to do it remotely; so, the person did not need to be in my proximity. But, I was tentative about exposing my ability to anyone else, still worried about scepticism.

I spent the lockdowns talking and counselling others I

knew and those referred to me, online via Zoom. The more I spoke to others, the more attuned I became to my channelling abilities, and people were suggesting that I needed to develop my psychic abilities. But I kept diverting my energies into counselling and advising others. Then I was approached by someone I had met at one of my conferences, and they invited me to use my counselling talents and experience, to work for the United Nations.

Once again, my connections had led me in a new and intriguing direction. I realised that my life had been guided in so many different directions, which were now finally converging to my ultimate true life purpose of helping others.

It's a beautiful thing to have new opportunities in life and a new destiny unfolding before my very eyes. I can't wait to discover what lies ahead and tell you about it in my next book.

I guess it was a blessing that I saw life from both sides. If life gave me hope, then death gave me purpose. After all, life and death really are just two sides of the same coin. I believe that if I never went through those years of illness or had those clashes with death, I would not be the person that I am today.

Life is fast and it is fleeting. It is hard, but it is also beautiful.

RITA'S PARTING PHILOSOPHY

There is magic to be found in every moment of the day, all you have to do is look for it. A smile is the best accessory you can wear: it shines and does not cost you a thing. Use it and wear it with pride.

You must have faith. This doesn't have to be in the traditional religious sense. You need to have faith in something or someone so that you can move forward in a positive way.

Treat yourself with care and compassion. When the mind, heart and gut are in sync, you will find that life is always going to head you in a positive direction. For you to be able to love

PART 3

what you do and do what you love, you must accept and love yourself first.

Most importantly, live every day like it could be your last. Live with love in your heart and passion in your soul. If you don't like something – change it. It is your life to take control of.

So, what are you waiting for?
Just do it!

Rita is sharing more in her INTERACTIVE book.

See exclusive downloads, videos, audios and photos.

DOWNLOAD it now at
www.deanpublishing.com/magicandmiracles

About the Author

Rita Barbagallo, 'The Red Peacock', is an international speaker and coach, celebrated author and philanthropy consultant, highly-acclaimed magician and business entrepreneur.

She is the founder of:
- Barbee Barb Children's Entertainment, established 1991
- Barbee Barb Magic School, established 1995
- Barbee Barb Collection, established 2014

She is the Australian HerStory Circle Curator and Director, and sits on the HerStory Circle Global Steering Committee.

When not speaking or writing books, Rita supports and volunteers for: The Red Cross, Sylvanvale Autistic School, St George and Sutherland Medical Research Foundation, World Vision, St George Hospital, Calvary Hospital, Westmead Children's Hospital and more.

ABOUT THE AUTHOR

ABOUT THE AUTHOR

Contact Rita @
www.barbeebarb.com.au
www.theredpeacock.com.au
www.thered-peacock.com
Facebook: Rita Barbagallo "The Red Peacock"
Address: PO Box 2, Sans Souci NSW 2219 Australia

Support services
If you are in Australia and are currently suffering from anxiety, depression or are in crisis, contact one of the hotlines listed below.

Beyond Blue
24-hour hotline:1300 22 4636

Blue Knot Foundation Helpline
9 am to 5 pm, 7 days a week: 1300 657 380

Kids Helpline
24-hour hotline: 1800 55 1800.

Lifeline
24-hour hotline: 13 11 14

Suicide Call Back Service
24-hour hotline: 1300 659 467

If you or someone you know is struggling with endometriosis, visit www.endometriosisaustralia.org to connect with your nearest support group.

Find your mission.

Be a princess every day!

A cave life can also be glamorous.

I'm a country girl in a Barbee world!

Don't worry about time, it will always follow you anyway.

Life is a highway, I want to ride it all night long.

Even on a bad day you can look fabulous – just put on your shades!

It's okay to take a little time out in the middle of the day.

Where else would you want to live?!

If the humans don't cut it, man's best friend always will.

When life puts you off balance, find something to lean on.

www.ingramcontent.com/pod-product-compliance
Lightning Source LLC
Chambersburg PA
CBHW041139110526
44590CB00027B/4074